LIFE ON EARTH
IN THE SEA

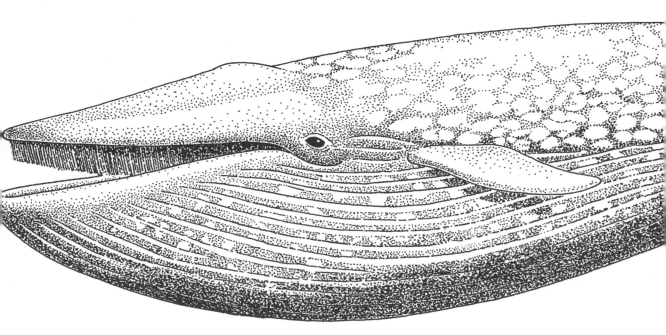

THE DIAGRAM GROUP

Facts On File, Inc.

Life On Earth: In the Sea

Written, edited, and produced by Diagram Visual Information Ltd

Editorial director:	Denis Kennedy
Editors:	Bender Richardson White, Gordon Lee
Contributor:	John Stidworthy
Indexer:	Martin Hargreaves
Art director:	Roger Kohn
Senior designer:	Lee Lawrence
Designers:	Anthony Atherton, Christian Owens
Illustrators:	Cecilia Fitzsimons, Kathleen McDougall, Sean Milne, Coral Mula, Graham Rosewarne
Picture researcher:	Neil McKenna

Facts On File, Inc.
132 West 31st Street
New York NY 10001

For Library of Congress Cataloging-in-Publication Data, please contact Facts On File, Inc.
ISBN 0-8160-5048-1

Facts On File books are available at special discounts when purchased in bulk quantities for businesses, associations, institutions, or sales promotions. Please call our Special Sales Department in New York at 212/967-8800 or 800/322-8755.

You can find Facts On File on the World Wide Web at: http://www.factsonfile.com

Printed in the United States of America

EB Diagram   10   9   8   7   6   5   4   3   2   1

This book is printed on acid-free paper.

Contents

Introduction

THIS BOOK is a concise, illustrated guide to living things that evolved in, and now inhabit, seas, oceans, rivers, lakes, and ponds. Texts, explanatory diagrams, illustrations, captions, and feature boxes combine to help readers grasp important information. A glossary clarifies the more difficult scientific terms for younger students, while a list of websites provides links to other relevant sources of additional information.

Chapter 1, *Water as a Place to Live*, examines the extent of the seas, how rivers and lakes are formed, and reviews the creatures that evolved to live in these habitats.

Chapter 2, *Animals without Backbones*, looks at the evolution of the first aquatic animals, from ancient sponges to crabs and krill, and also focuses on the evolution of mollusks, ranging from ammonites to modern squid.

Chapter 3, *Fishes and Amphibians*, describes the evolution and progression of the first animals with a backbone, from ancient sharks to salamanders, toads, and frogs.

Chapter 4, *Aquatic Reptiles*, looks at prehistoric animals ranging from placodonts and plesiosaurs to ichthyosaurs, and describes modern reptiles that spend time in water.

Chapter 5, *Water Mammals*, features whales, dolphins, seals, and sea lions, which spend their time in seawater, and freshwater animals such as shrews, voles, and the duckbill platypus.

Chapter 6, *Waterbirds*, describes the variety of winged creatures that spend part of their lives beside, in, on, or under water.

Chapter 7, *Water Environments*, looks at various marine and freshwater habitats, and how living things adapt to them.

Chapter 8, *Migration*, focuses on the variety of marine and freshwater animals that regularly travel great distances through seas and oceans, or along rivers.

In the Sea is one of six titles in the Life On Earth series that looks at the evolution and diversity of our planet, its features, and living things, both past and present.

The series features all life-forms, from bacteria and algae to trees and mammals. It also highlights the infinite variety of adaptations and strategies for survival among living things, and describes different habitats, how they evolved, and the communities of creatures that inhabit them. Individual chapters discuss the characteristics of specific taxonomic groups of living things, or types of landscape, or planetary features.

Life On Earth has been written by natural history experts and is generously illustrated with line drawings, labeled diagrams, and maps. The series provides students with a solid, necessary foundation for their future studies in science.

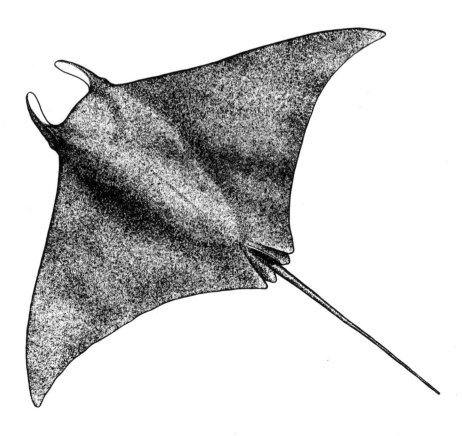

⑥ Size of the seas

Seas provide more living space than on land. Oceans cover 70 percent of the Earth's surface. The deepest parts are further down than the height of the tallest mountains on land. Mount Everest would disappear if dropped into the ocean depths.

AS WELL AS PROVIDING a huge area of seabed on which animals can live, the sea has a surface which can provide a place for swimming or floating animals, and all the water in between seabed and surface can be used by swimming creatures.

Although for millennia humans have used the sea to travel or fish, most see just a tiny part of its surface waters. The depths are out of sight and, even today, almost unknown. Only very tough, expensive craft, such as the submersible "Alvin," can penetrate into the deep, dark waters. When such machines explore, either with humans on board, or as remote-controlled robots, they often find new, unexpected forms of life. Sometimes these look— to land-based animals such as us—totally bizarre. In the vastness of the sea live the largest animals known, and also many of the smallest. Some creatures, such as tuna fish, exist in huge shoals. Enormous swarms of copepods (tiny shrimp-like creatures) make them among the most numerous animals on Earth. Other creatures are known from just a single specimen that has been found. Are these really very rare, or do they just live in a part of the ocean that we have been unable to explore so far?

The sea was home to much of the early life on our planet, and still contains a huge variety of life.

Lights

ALVIN

Propellers

Viewing ports

"Alvin"
Deep-diving submersibles must withstand much greater differences in pressure than spacecraft.

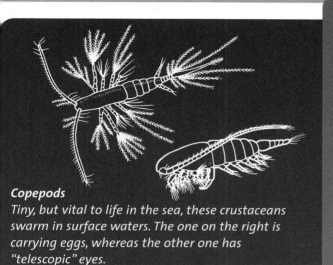

Copepods
Tiny, but vital to life in the sea, these crustaceans swarm in surface waters. The one on the right is carrying eggs, whereas the other one has "telescopic" eyes.

IT'S A FACT!
The Pacific is the most extensive ocean in the world, covering 64 million square miles (166 million sq km). It features the deepest known spot—the Marianas Trench—at 35,797 feet (10,911 m) below sea level. The Pacific Ocean also contains more water than the Atlantic, Indian, and Arctic Oceans combined.

Marianas Trench

Pacific Ocean

The continental shelf extends from the edge of a continent, making the sea there comparatively shallow—about 600 feet (180 m) deep. At its edge, the sea bottom drops down to the abyssal plain, about 13,000 feet (4,000 m) deep, forming most of the ocean floor. In a few places the seabed plunges to deep trenches. In other places volcanoes rise from the seabed. Some reach the surface, but others remain submerged. There are chains of submarine mountains, too, up to 6,000 feet (1,800 m) high, running across the seabed in mid-ocean.

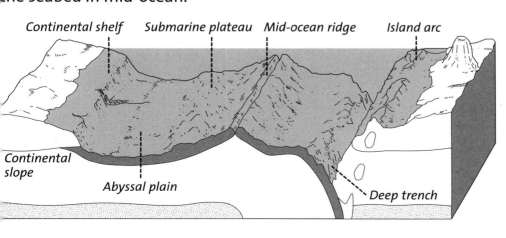

Continental shelf   Submarine plateau   Mid-ocean ridge   Island arc

Continental slope

Abyssal plain

Deep trench

The ocean floor
This illustration shows an imaginary, but "typical," cross-section of ocean floor between two continents, with its plains, mountains, and trenches.

©DIAGRAM

The seas contain 97.29 percent of the world's water. A tiny amount (0.014 percent) is in freshwater rivers, lakes and ponds. Over forty times as much is actually in the ground (0.605 percent). About 2.09 percent is bound up in ice caps and glaciers. Only about 0.001 percent exists in the air as water vapor.

WATER IS ALWAYS circulating between the sea and the land. Water also evaporates from the sea and land. As water vapor cools over mountains, for example, clouds form and drops of water fall as rain, snow, or hail. The water may soak into the ground, but when water meets an impermeable layer it can go no lower, and emerges from the ground as a spring. More water running off the land adds to this and a stream forms. On lower ground, this may become a river, which then returns water to the sea through an estuary. Or water may become trapped in a basin as a pond or lake.

The water cycle
Water evaporates from the land and is transpired by plants. The same water is returned to the ground when rain or snow falls.

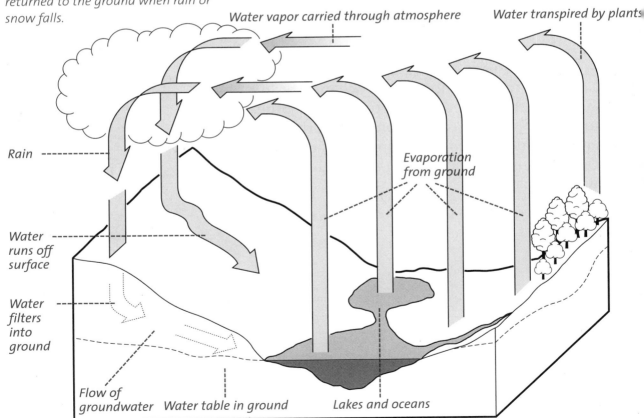

Water vapor carried through atmosphere

Water transpired by plants

Rain

Evaporation from ground

Water runs off surface

Water filters into ground

Flow of groundwater   Water table in ground   Lakes and oceans

Although small compared to the oceans, the fresh waters of the world are so varied that they provide many types of habitats for wildlife, and a huge number of species inhabit them. From the fastest torrent to completely still water, from glacial lakes to the hottest springs, from the tiniest pond or stream to lakes covering hundreds of square miles (square kilometers), there are animals living.

The largest lake in area in the world is Superior in North America, which covers 31,700 square miles (82,103 sq km), followed by Victoria in Africa at 26,826 square miles (69,479 sq km). No lake approaches the depths of the deepest oceans, but Baikal in Asia is the deepest at 5,315 feet (1,620 m), followed by Tanganyika in Africa at 4,708 feet (1,435 m). Superior, with an average depth of 1,330 feet (405 m), is comparatively shallow, and Victoria averages only 270 feet (82 m) deep. Baikal, with a volume of 12,250 cubic miles (51,030 cu km), contains the most water of any freshwater lake.

THE WORLD'S LONGEST RIVERS

Nile
4,160 miles
(6,695 km)

Amazon
4,000 miles
(6,437 km)

Yangtze
3,964 miles
(6,379 km)

Mississippi-Missouri
3,740 miles
(6,019 km)

3,500 miles

3,000 miles

The Great Lakes
The five largest lakes in the group are shown (below left).

Lake Superior
31,700 square miles
(82,103 sq km)

Lake Huron
23,000 square miles
(59,570 sq km)

Lake Ontario
7,550 square miles
(19,554 sq km)

Lake Michigan
22,300 square miles
(57,757 sq km)

Lake Erie
9,910 square miles
(25,667 sq km)

© DIAGRAM

Most of the first living things we know about lived in the oceans. Even today, water is the largest component of animal bodies, and many animals have body fluids with a similar concentration of chemicals to that of seawater.

GROUPS OF ANIMALS, such as the starfish, sponges, and corals evolved in the water and always lived there. Other groups, such as mollusks, started as marine animals, and most still are, but some members, such as snails, moved to land or fresh water. Among the vertebrates (backboned animals) by far the biggest number are fishes living in water. The other groups of vertebrates are generally considered land animals, with amphibians just going into water to breed. In fact there are some types of amphibian that have gone back to being full-time water animals. Modern reptiles have plenty of aquatic types and, going back hundreds of millions of years, you can find reptiles that were completely adapted for a sea life. Mammals and birds, too, have plenty of examples, both fossil and present day, of partly or fully aquatic species.

The seas provided the conditions for the first animal life hundreds of millions of years ago. From these early animals all the other types evolved. The seas came to contain an enormously complex web of life. Animals developed with very different body plans and ways of life. The exact mix of animals has changed over time. Some kinds of animal that were once successful, such as trilobites, are now extinct. Newer animals have filled the space. But other kinds of animal, such as lampshells, have managed to continue unchanged for 500 million years.

Lampshells (above)
These are 500 million years old.

Stalkless feather stars (above)
These evolved 200 million years ago.

Aquatic animals (right)
This chart shows some of the main groups of aquatic animals and the periods during which they first appeared, or lived.

Millions of years ago	Period	Who lived at that time?		
65–present	Tertiary and Quaternary	Whale	Teleost bony fish	Penguin
144–65	Cretaceous	Starfish	Crocodilian	Mosasaur
206–144	Jurassic	Ammonite	Ichthyosaur	Plesiosaur
248–206	Triassic	Froglike amphibian	Placodont	Nothosaur
290–248	Permian	King crab	"Amphibian"	Mesosaur
354–290	Carboniferous	Chondrichthyan	Acanthodian	"Amphibian"
417–354	Devonian	Placoderm	Chondrichthyan	Bony fish
443–417	Silurian	Eurypterid	Jawless fish	Annelid worm
490–443	Ordovician	Nautiloid mollusk	Brachiopod	Sea lily
543–490	Cambrian	Mollusk	Trilobite	Lancelet
2,500–543	Proterozoic periods	Ediacaria	Spriggina	Sea pen

© DIAGRAM

It is difficult for soft-bodied animals to become preserved as fossils in the rocks. Their bodies usually decay soon after death. Over time, rocks may wear away, become heated, or crushed. It is therefore rare for fossils of soft-bodied animals.

AT EDIACARA, AUSTRALIA, in rocks formed 560 million years ago, the unusual has happened. Fossils of soft-bodied animals are preserved well enough for study. Many are so different from creatures living now that it is difficult to understand what they were, and how they worked. Others are enough like animals we know today for us to be fairly sure what they were. They lived in a shallow sea and were preserved in the beach sand. Hundreds of specimens exist, some of which are very detailed.

Life was already varied. We can probably recognize jellyfish, sponges, animals resembling present-day soft corals called sea pens, and various wormlike creatures, such as *Spriggina*.

The real "explosion" of life took place in the Cambrian period, from 543 to 490 million years ago. In the early Cambrian, several types of animals developed hard skeletons or shells that gave them a new means of protection. These also provided something for muscles to be attached to, allowing new ways of moving and feeding. Skeletons allowed life to expand dramatically.

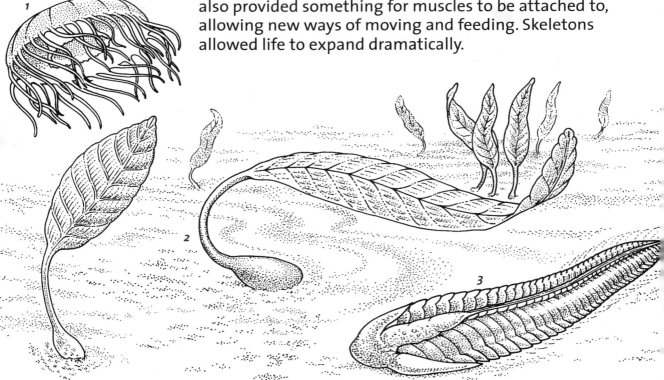

Nearly all the main divisions of animal life had evolved: corals, sponges, worms, early mollusks, lampshells, and echinoderms. There were even primitive chordates, animals that gave rise to backboned animals, and eventually, human beings. Many of these animals differed from later relatives in many details, but basic body plans were already fixed. A few extra groups, with bodies unlike any modern animal, lived in the Cambrian period then died out.

Arthropods were first seen in the Cambrian period. These are an important group of animals with jointed legs that later produced the insects that are such a success on land. But the first numerous and successful arthropods were the sea-dwelling trilobites. As the name suggests, these animals had three lobes to their bodies: one central, and one on each side. They had a series of segments, each of which had paired Y-shaped, jointed legs. They used the lower arm of the Y for walking. The upper part carried a gill. The whole body was covered in a hard, limy skeleton that was regularly molted. (Molted skins were often fossilized.) The head section had a pair of compound eyes. Some trilobites had excellent vision.

While keeping the same type of body plan, trilobites diversified. They became crawlers, burrowers, and swimmers. Some hunted, others were filter feeders. Although successful in the Cambrian sea and for some time after, trilobites died out about 250 million years ago.

UNDER THE MICROSCOPE
Trilobites had eyes comprised of many compartments, up to 15,000 in some species. They had compound eyes millions of years before insects.

Ediacara
The fine sandstone of Ediacara was laid down in shallow water, and preserved the outline of ancient soft-bodied animals, such as:
1 *"Jellyfish"*
2 *Sea-pens*
3 *Spriggina*
4 *Dickinsonia*
5 *Tube-worm*
6 *Sea anemone*

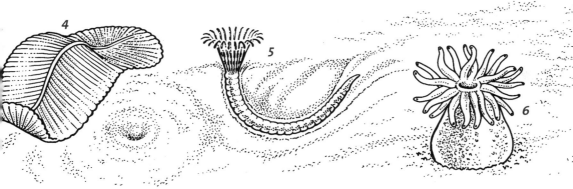

© DIAGRAM

In warm seas, coral reefs fringe the shore. Although built by small animals, some are huge. The Great Barrier Reef stretches nearly 1,333 miles (2,140 km) down the east coast of Australia. Reefs have been growing in the seas for over 500 million years, but it has not always been the same types of animals (or other organisms) that have made them.

BACK IN THE CAMBRIAN PERIOD, reefs grew in shallow waters. Primitive sponges called archaeocyaths were the first building blocks. These cone-shaped, or flattened, animals drew water through their bodies to trap food. They had a supporting skeleton made of calcium carbonate. Most were under an inch (2 cm) tall, but some grew to a size of 3 feet (1 m). Around them grew cyanobacteria, each one microscopic, but able to lay down calcium carbonate. So many grew that there could be a solid pile several yards (meters) thick.

This simple reef provided a home where other animals could live. Trilobites hunted through it. Early relatives of starfish, not at all starfish-shaped, perched on the reef and filtered the water for food. Primitive lampshells, which were also filter feeders, sat in crevices.

Archaeocyath sponges died out quite soon. In the next period (Ordovician—490 to 443 million years ago) new kinds of animals helped build reefs. More complex reefs formed.

A reef often started when sea lilies colonized the sea floor. These echinoderms look like feathery starfish on stalks, and have a skeleton made of hard plates. The stalk is a series of rings. The sea lilies, and their dead skeletons, provided a foundation. Sponges, some with glassy skeletons, others with massive calcium carbonate skeletons, helped build the reef.

Cyanobacteria were still prevalent. Before the end of the Ordovician period, little mat-forming animals known as bryozoans had joined in, as well as the first real corals.

Silurian coral
Fossil skeletons of corals have been found exclusively in reefs in one area of Britain. The different species can be recognized by the contrasting patterns that were made by their colonies.

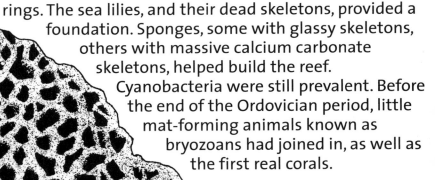

Between 443 and 417 million years ago, in the Silurian period, reef building was at a peak. Sponges were important building blocks, but early types of corals were also important. Corals were often solitary, each a little like a sea anemone encased in a thick skeleton. Some formed branching groups that helped build the reef.

Another type of coral, the tabulates, formed big colonies with fan-shaped or chain-like skeletons. The reef held other animals, including lampshells and bryozoans. Close by lived more active animals such as trilobites, early cephalopods (squid relatives) and the early fish-like animals.

IT'S A FACT
Sea lilies lived successfully, and in abundance, in both shallow and deep seas for hundreds of millions of years. Nowadays only a small number remain, living in the ocean depths.

Silurian reef
Reefs housed many animals, which included:
1 Crinoids (sea lilies)
2 Corals
3 Trilobites
4 Sponges
5 Nautiloids (early squid relative)

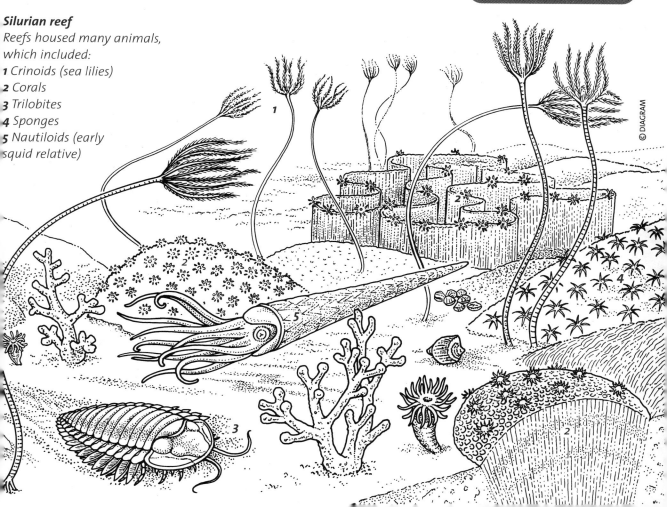

© DIAGRAM

Familiar crustaceans include crabs, lobsters, and shrimps. There are 40,000 species of crustacean, most of them living in the sea. Crustaceans are known from well over 500 million years ago.

CRUSTACEANS have segmented bodies, with two-branched jointed legs, and often a hard carapace (shell) over the head end. The legs may be adapted for walking, swimming, or catching prey, and often bear gills for breathing. Body and limb shapes are modified in very different ways. Crabs, for example, have big claws to catch prey. Other crustaceans are specialized as parasites. Others rake in the "plant life" of the sea.

Crustaceans have played an important part in sea life. In ancient times, tiny crustaceans provided food for bigger animals. Larger crustaceans burrowed down into mud on the sea floor, turning it over and aerating it. Today, crustaceans are still important, particularly some of the smaller species that are key components of the ocean food chain.

The floating or weakly swimming animals or plants in the top layers of the ocean are called plankton. Many tiny planktonic animals are crustaceans. Some are larvae. Crabs float in the plankton when tiny larvae, then change shape and move to the sea bottom as adults. Barnacles, too, have typical crustacean floating larvae before attaching to a rock as adults.

Many crustaceans spend their lives in the plankton. Copepods are tiny, often only 0.04–0.08 inches (1–2 mm), but make up 70 percent of the plankton animals. They are probably the most numerous animals on Earth. They use their legs to pull tiny plants to their mouths. In turn, many other animals in the plankton eat them. So the copepods are at the base of the animal food chain in the sea. Other plankton, fish, and larger animals, depend on them.

Plankton
Among a mixture of single-celled, and larger, animals and plants, crustaceans are often prominent members of the plankton.

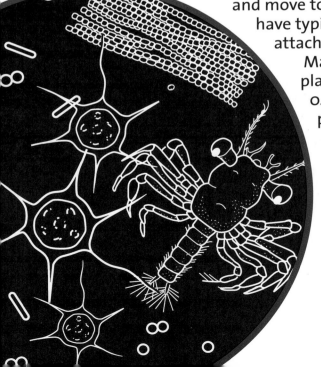

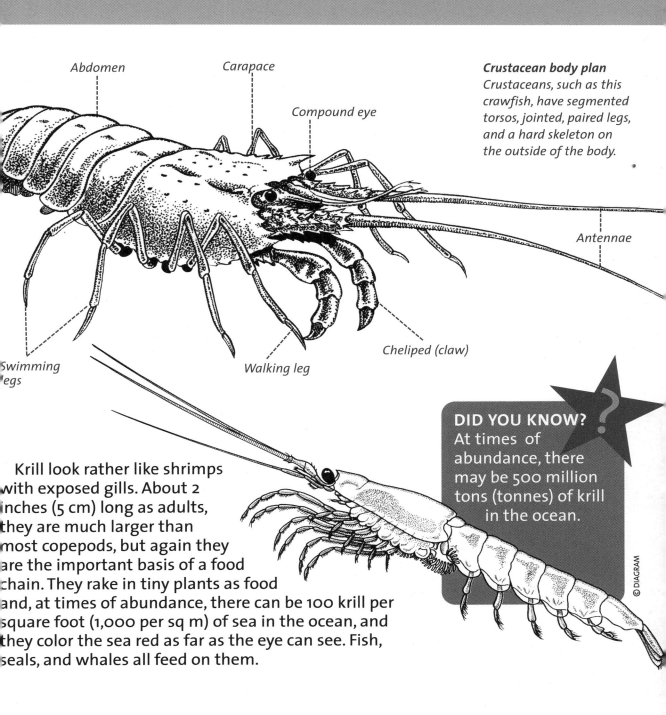

Abdomen

Carapace

Compound eye

Crustacean body plan
Crustaceans, such as this crawfish, have segmented torsos, jointed, paired legs, and a hard skeleton on the outside of the body.

Antennae

Cheliped (claw)

Swimming legs

Walking leg

DID YOU KNOW?
At times of abundance, there may be 500 million tons (tonnes) of krill in the ocean.

Krill look rather like shrimps with exposed gills. About 2 inches (5 cm) long as adults, they are much larger than most copepods, but again they are the important basis of a food chain. They rake in tiny plants as food and, at times of abundance, there can be 100 krill per square foot (1,000 per sq m) of sea in the ocean, and they color the sea red as far as the eye can see. Fish, seals, and whales all feed on them.

© DIAGRAM

The mollusks are a group that includes snails, mussels, and octopuses. Most have an outside shell rather than an internal skeleton, and an unsegmented body. They breathe through gills and have a fold of skin, called the mantle, that encloses the internal organs. The mouth of gastropod mollusks like snails has a radula, a long tongue covered in rasping teeth. It moves on a single muscular "foot."

THE BASIC MOLLUSK body plan is ancient, dating back to around 530 million years ago. One of the most primitive living mollusks is called *Neopilina*. Unlike most mollusks, it has repeated pairs of body organs, such as gills and excretory organs, perhaps a clue that mollusks, like insects and crustaceans, evolved from segmented animals. Animals like *Neopilina* are found as fossils in ancient rocks, but were thought to have died out about 400 million years ago. In the middle of the last century, though, living specimens were fished out of the deep ocean trenches. *Neopilina* is believed to crawl on the sea floor finding tiny food particles.

After the insects, the mollusks are perhaps the most successful group of animals, with about 75,000 species. Snails and whelks, with their coiled shells, form the majority of the modern mollusks, but up until 70 million years ago there were relatively few species. Bivalves,

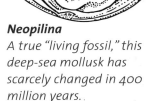

Neopilina
A true "living fossil," this deep-sea mollusk has scarcely changed in 400 million years.

Anatomy of a snail
The main body organs of a snail.

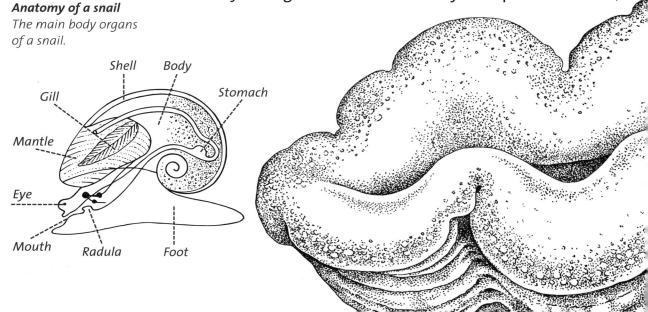

Shell
Body
Stomach
Gill
Mantle
Eye
Mouth
Radula
Foot

such as clams and cephalopods, were more common.

Bivalves have a double shell which they close tight for protection. Nearly all stay in one place as adults, or move about very slowly, but like other mollusks their larvae are free-swimming in the plankton. As well as breathing with their gills, bivalves use them to trap particles of food. Most bivalves are quite small, but the giant clams of the tropics are huge.

Many types of bivalve we have today—oysters, scallops, mussels—can be recognized in rocks from the time of the dinosaurs. Sometimes the borings of ancient "shipworm" bivalves can be recognized in fossil wood. Other bivalves were unlike any today. The rudists grew on reefs and were attached at the base by one cone-shaped shell. The other shell made a cap over the end of the cone. Some rudists were 3 feet (1 m) tall.

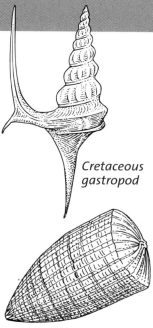

Cretaceous gastropod

Rudist

IT'S A FACT
A giant clam may be 4 feet (1.2 m) across, with a shell that weighs 440 pounds (200 kg).

Fossil shells (right)
Mollusk shells fossilize well. Shells, such as Cretaceous gastropods and scallops, exist little changed since the dinosaur era. Rudists and "Devil's toenail" oysters are extinct.

"Devil's toenail" oyster

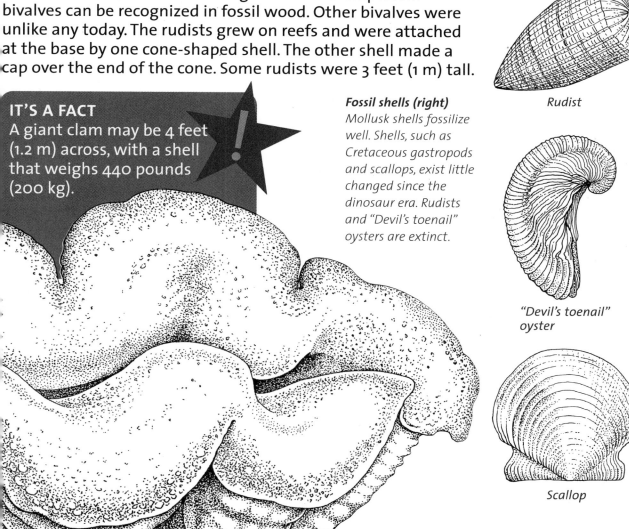

Scallop

© DIAGRAM

Some mollusks, such as nautiloids, grew a shell with a series of chambers. The main body of the animal was in the last chamber, exposed to the water. Its head, with sense organs, and its "foot," divided into tentacles, protruded. The nautiloids are known from over 500 million years ago, but became very common from about 450 million years ago.

IT'S A FACT
The eye of a nautilus is very simple, with no lens, and works like a pinhole camera.

CEPHALOPODS are all hunters. Early nautiloids had shells in the shape of a long thin cone. Many were small, but some grew as large as 11 feet (3.4 m) long, the biggest animals of their time. Later nautiloids developed coiled shells.

One type, the pearly nautilus, survives in the seas today: its shell, with many gas-filled chambers, acts as a buoyancy aid. Its beak is surrounded by many suckerless tentacles. A pair of eyes peers from under a hood that shuts down when the animal retreats into its shell. The sense organs and nervous system are poorly developed,

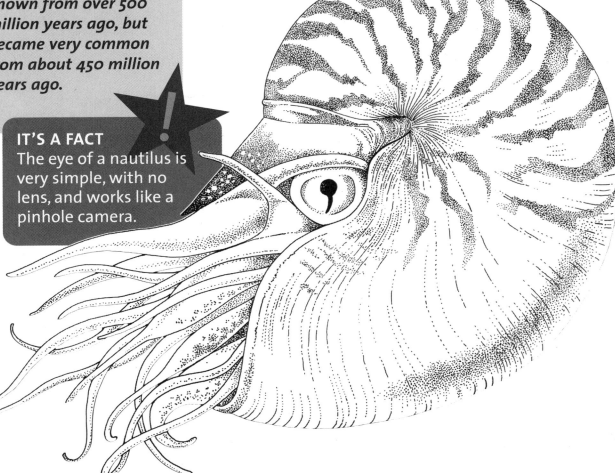

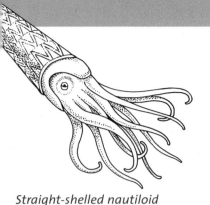

Straight-shelled nautiloid

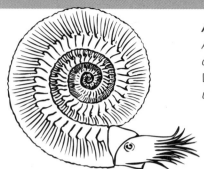

Stephanoceras

Ammonites
Ammonite shells were usually coiled and ornamented like Douvilleiceras, *but some had an uncoiled horn shape like* Hamites.

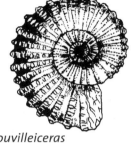

Douvilleiceras

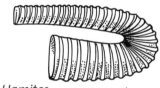

Hamites

...nd a nautilus looks like an old-fashioned design, as it is in ...omparison with some other cephalopods.

In the ancient seas, about 350 million years ago, ammonites ...egan to take over from the nautiloids. Their shells showed ...imilarities to that of nautilus, but they came in a variety of ...hapes, the coiled varieties being most common. The fossil ...hells show amazing elaboration of the walls between the ...hambers of the shell. As a result of fast evolution, with new ...pecies and shell types every million years or so, a fossil ...mmonite can identify a rock layer with great precision. In ...pite of their huge success in the seas from 250 to 65 million ...ears ago, ammonites all died out at ...he same time as the dinosaurs.

The ancient cephalopods most ...losely related to present-day squids ...vere the belemnites. These had a ...hell inside the body, rather than ...urrounding it, and were agile ...wimmers. Although evolving earlier, ...hey were successful in the time of ...he dinosaurs but, unlike ammonites, ... few kinds survived them for a while. ...arge numbers of belemnite shells are ...ometimes found together, and they ...nay have hunted together in shoals.

BACK IN TIME
A few fossil belemnites have been found with impressions of soft parts in the rock. They had ten arms armed with suckers, and horny hooks for catching prey. Even the ink sac may be visible.

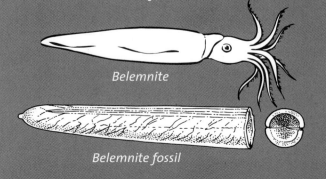

Belemnite

Belemnite fossil

© DIAGRAM

Among animals without backbones, the living cephalopods include the biggest, fastest-swimming, and the brainiest. The shell that was so prominent in ancient cephalopods is much reduced. Cuttlefish have an internal shell (the cuttlefish "bone" which is given to cage birds) full of gas that helps to regulate buoyancy. True squids have just a thin membranous shell remnant inside, and octopuses have no shell.

CUTTLEFISH are short and flattened and live on the sea bottom, although they can swim well. They include some of the fastest color changers among animals. They can use their colors for camouflage, but also use vivid patterns to attract mates or intimidate rivals. Tiny muscles change the shape of pigment cells in the skin. Change can be immediate, and a cuttlefish can send waves of pattern down its body. This all suggests a well-developed nervous system. This is also characteristic of modern squids and octopuses. They have large "brains" and fast-acting nerves. They have good eyes, and good organs of balance. The tentacles have sense cells that allow them to taste as well as feel textures. Most cephalopods have an "ink sac," where they store black pigment that can be puffed into the water when they are alarmed, leaving a distracting decoy while they make their escape.

Octopuses live on the sea bottom, or hide in rock crevices. They crawl

Common octopus

Suckers (left)
As well as being useful in grasping prey, suckers also serve as sense organs that can feel shapes and textures.

or swim well with their eight tentacles, or by using jet propulsion. They catch crabs and other animals with their tentacles and bite them with a horny beak. The giant Pacific octopus has tentacles that can span 16.5 feet (5 m) or more. Most octopuses are much smaller.

A predatory squid
Two big eyes, and two long arms with suckers, help the squid to seize prey.

Squids have streamlined bodies with fins at the side. They flap these to swim "tail" first or head first. They also shoot out a water jet to move quickly. Some are among the fastest swimmers in the sea, beaten only by a few large fish and whales. They are formidable hunters and fast enough to escape most enemies. Most squids live in the open sea. Some squids live very deep, including the biggest of all, the giant squid, which can grow to 70 feet (21 m) or more.

IT'S A FACT
The fastest squids have been clocked at 34 miles per hour (55 kmph). Some kinds can jump into the air and glide 150 feet (45 m).

Cephalopods (left)
Cuttlefish and octopuses live in shallow water. Vampire and giant squids live in the deep sea.

Vampire squid

Common cuttlefish

IT'S A FACT
Few octopuses are dangerous to people, but the tiny blue-ringed octopus of the western Pacific has a deadly poisonous bite.

Giant squid

© DIAGRAM

In the warm sea, a 2 inch (5 cm) long fish-shaped animal sits buried in the sand. Its front end sticks into the water. It sifts tiny food particles from the water, using its mouth tentacles and gills. This animal, the lancelet, is a simple one, but it has some features that might have been seen in the ancestors of fishes.

THE FIRST true backboned animals appear in rocks 470 million years old. These first fishes had no jaws, and like the modern lancelet sifted the water or scooped mud from the sea bottom. They had tail fins, but no paired fins as fish do today. What they did have, in abundance, was bone. Many of the jawless fishes of the next 100 million years had hard plates of bone over the head region and bony scales over other parts of the body. The backbone itself was made of cartilage. Some of these fishes had fleshy lobes or bony "wings" at the side that may have helped with stability.

Most ancient jawless fish were small, up to 8 inches (20 cm) long. Perhaps this is why armor was so useful.

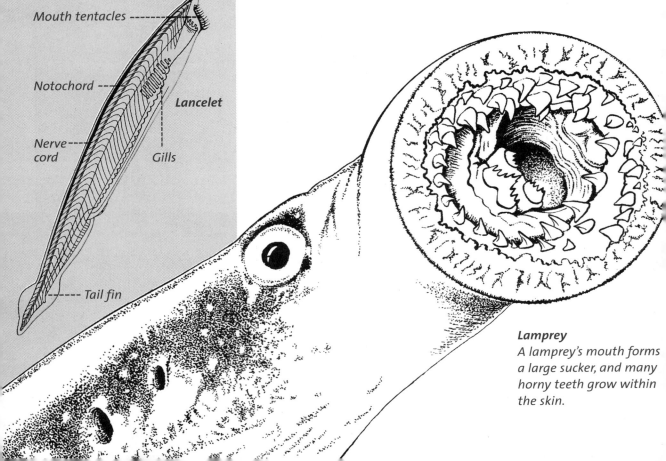

Mouth tentacles

Notochord

Lancelet

Nerve cord

Gills

Tail fin

Lamprey
A lamprey's mouth forms a large sucker, and many horny teeth grow within the skin.

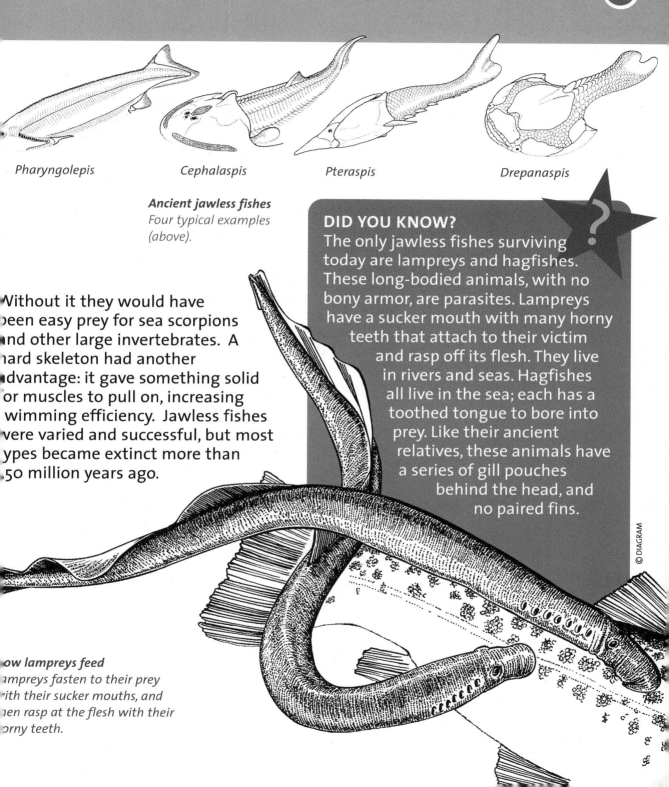

Pharyngolepis

Cephalaspis

Pteraspis

Drepanaspis

Ancient jawless fishes
Four typical examples (above).

DID YOU KNOW?
The only jawless fishes surviving today are lampreys and hagfishes. These long-bodied animals, with no bony armor, are parasites. Lampreys have a sucker mouth with many horny teeth that attach to their victim and rasp off its flesh. They live in rivers and seas. Hagfishes all live in the sea; each has a toothed tongue to bore into prey. Like their ancient relatives, these animals have a series of gill pouches behind the head, and no paired fins.

Without it they would have been easy prey for sea scorpions and other large invertebrates. A hard skeleton had another advantage: it gave something solid for muscles to pull on, increasing swimming efficiency. Jawless fishes were varied and successful, but most types became extinct more than 350 million years ago.

© DIAGRAM

How lampreys feed
Lampreys fasten to their prey with their sucker mouths, and then rasp at the flesh with their horny teeth.

PLACODERMS (the name means "plated skins") were heavily armored with bone. They lived from about 440 million years ago to 355 million years ago. Some were powerful swimmers, with two pairs of side fins and a strong tail. They developed into many different shapes and sizes. Some, such as *Bothriolepis*, were small, but had front fins covered in jointed armor, looking rather like crab claws. (Perhaps they used these fins to walk on the bottom of the sea, or even briefly on land.) Other placoderms had the shape expected of a fish. Some grew to enormous sizes, the biggest animals the world had seen, and were ferocious killers. The head was jointed. The top jaw could swing up, the lower jaw down, producing a big gape. The tail was generally sharklike.

DID YOU KNOW?
Large placoderms such as *Dunkleosteus* grew to 33 feet (10 m), which is longer than today's great white shark.

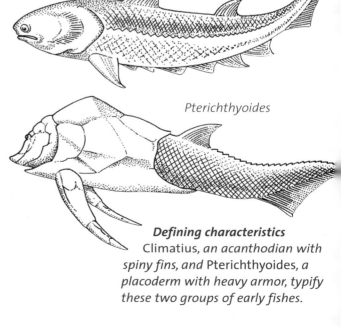

Climatius

Pterichthyoides

Defining characteristics
Climatius, *an acanthodian with spiny fins, and* Pterichthyoides, *a placoderm with heavy armor, typify these two groups of early fishes.*

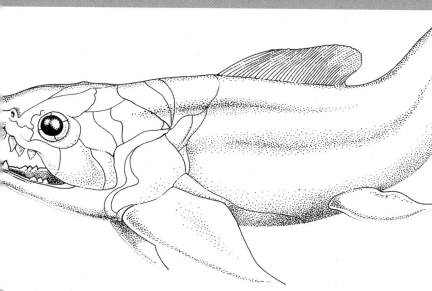

Placoderms
Even predatory placoderms like this lacked the maneuverability of modern fishes.

he placoderms, despite all their bony armor, may be the
istant relatives of sharks today.

Acanthodian fishes were abundant at the same time as the
lacoderms, but lasted longer, until about 280 million years
go. Sometimes called "spiny sharks," they were very spiny,
ut were not sharks. They had a shark-shaped asymmetrical
il, an anal fin below, one or two dorsal fins above, a pair of
ns (pectorals) at the front, and
pair (pelvics) further back. The
ns had long spines at the front,
d there were sometimes
dditional rows of spines along
e belly.

Acanthodians had big eyes,
obably important for hunting.
ost seem to have been quite
nall, about 8 inches (20 cm)
ng, but some grew to 6 feet
m), with formidable jaws.
thers lost their teeth and used
eir gills to filter the water for
od.

**STRANGE
BUT TRUE!**
Acanthodian
fishes had a
fixed number of
scales. These
kept pace with
their growth
throughout their
lifespan.

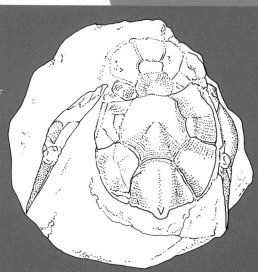

Placoderm fossil
*A block of rock
shows the head
and bony flipper
like pectoral fins of
Bothriolepis,
a fish similar to
Pterichthyoides.
These fins may
have helped it to
"walk" and also
to dig itself into
the mud.*

©DIAGRAM

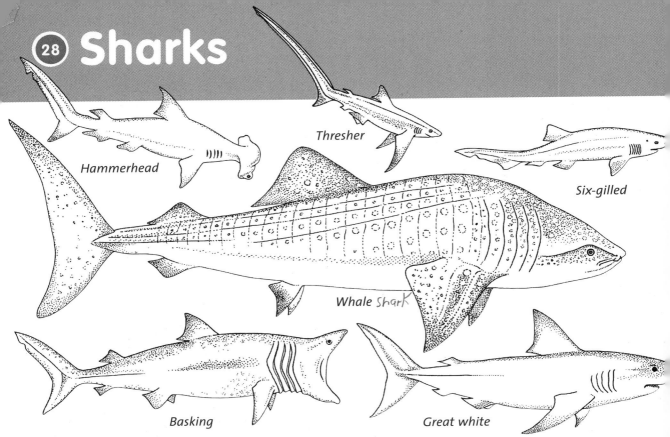

Hammerhead

Thresher

Six-gilled

Whale Shark

Basking

Great white

Sharks have a skeleton made of cartilage. They lost the bony armor found in many early fishes. The skin is protected by little tooth-shaped scales. These, and the teeth themselves, are the hardest parts of the body.
Teeth are the parts most easily fossilized and most common to turn up in the fossil record.
Sharks have stiff pectoral and pelvic fins, useful as stabilizers, but less so for steering and braking. Most are denser than water and need to keep swimming to stay upright.

SHARKS ARE KNOWN to have existed for th[e] last 400 million years, through times whe[n] large numbers of other animals died out. I[n] some ways, with their row of gill slits, stiff fins, and unevenly lobed tail, sharks appear primitive little changed from their remote ancestors. But although there are only about 360 species, compared to thousands of bony fish, the sharks include many of the biggest fish. Their senses, streamlined shape, teeth, and other adaptation[s] equip them to be top predators.

Sharks are basically egg-layers, but some species keep the eggs inside their bodies until hatching. Some even provide a nourishing liqui[d] "milk" for developing young inside the body. Some of the large sharks, such as mako sharks and the great white, can maintain a high body temperature compared to their surroundings, s[o] can be very active. A mako has been timed

SHARK FILE
★ *Tiger* (20 feet, 6 m)
Eats almost anything.
★ *Great white* (26 feet, 8 m)
Preys on seals, dolphins, other animals, and occasionally people.
★ *Hammerhead* (16 feet, 5 m)
Hunter, helped by electrically sensitive organs in its wide snout.
★ *Thresher* (20 feet, 6 m)
Predator, uses tail to stun smaller fish.
★ *Basking* (32–50 feet, 10–15 m) Filter feeder.
★ *Whale* (40–60 feet, 12–18 m) Filter feeder.
★ *Spiny pygmy* (10 inches, 25 cm)
Small, deep-water shark.

swimming at 60 miles per hour (95 kmph). Mako and great white sharks have probably existed almost unchanged, judging by their fossil teeth, for 100 million years. Some living sharks, such as the six-gilled shark (most sharks have only five gills) might have stayed the same for twice as long. The huge teeth of the big predatory sharks are formidable weapons, but the largest sharks of all, such as basking sharks, feed on plankton and have no use for teeth, which are tiny. Their gills act as filters to trap food.

BACK IN TIME
A shark has up to 600 teeth in its mouth at once, which are constantly being replaced. Thousands may be lost during its lifetime.

DID YOU KNOW?
Fossil shark scales are found further back in time than their teeth. Did sharks develop toothed jaws after their scaly covering?

Fossil tooth
Shark teeth are very hard and durable, as evidenced by this relic.

© DIAGRAM

Rays and skates have pectoral fins that spread to form large "wings" for swimming. Many live on, or near, the bottom of the sea. They have gill slits facing downward. These act as exits for water used in breathing. Rays draw water into the gills from the spiracle—a hole at the back of the top of the head—and have small, tooth-shaped scales.

SOME SPECIES, such as thornback rays, have large scales down the back for protection. The teeth of most rays have been turned into flat plates for grinding and crushing food, such as mollusks and crabs.

In the sea today there are as many kinds of ray as shark. The two related groups developed their own specializations at least 200 million years ago. By about 100 million years ago, there were already skates, stingrays, and sawfishes similar to modern species.

Sawfishes have wide bodies, but a long snout with sharp teeth on each side. It is used as a weapon to slash into a shoal of fish before the sawfish eats its victims. Typical rays and skates live on the bottom and feed on slow-moving prey. They lay large shelled eggs ("mermaid's purses") that are sometimes washed up on shore. Electric rays have very round bodies without a scaly covering. They can protect themselves with electric shocks that are also used to stun prey. Stingrays

"Mermaid's purse" A ray may develop for many months inside the tough leathery shell before hatching.

IT'S A FACT
The Pacific manta ray can have a "wingspan" of 20 feet (6 m), and weigh 1.6 tons (tonnes).

Manta ray

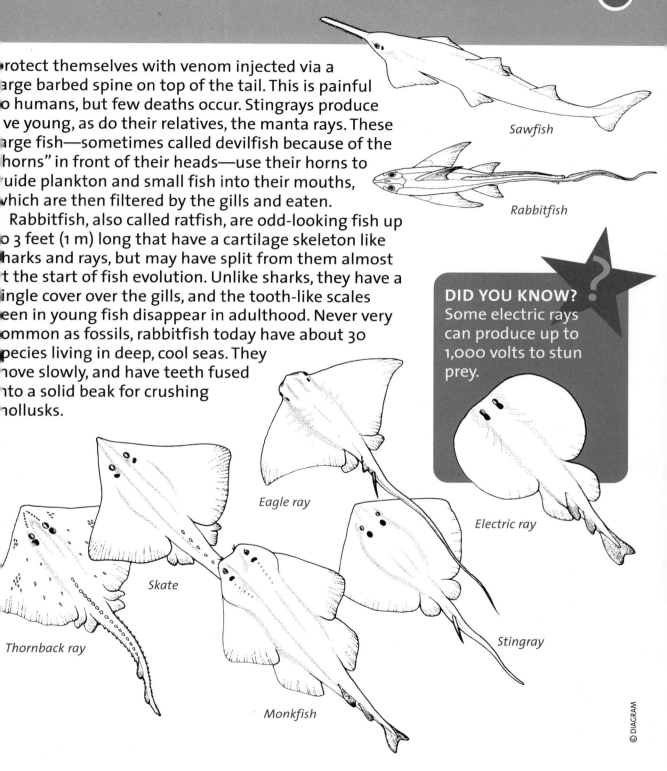

protect themselves with venom injected via a large barbed spine on top of the tail. This is painful to humans, but few deaths occur. Stingrays produce live young, as do their relatives, the manta rays. These large fish—sometimes called devilfish because of the "horns" in front of their heads—use their horns to guide plankton and small fish into their mouths, which are then filtered by the gills and eaten.

Rabbitfish, also called ratfish, are odd-looking fish up to 3 feet (1 m) long that have a cartilage skeleton like sharks and rays, but may have split from them almost at the start of fish evolution. Unlike sharks, they have a single cover over the gills, and the tooth-like scales seen in young fish disappear in adulthood. Never very common as fossils, rabbitfish today have about 30 species living in deep, cool seas. They move slowly, and have teeth fused into a solid beak for crushing mollusks.

Sawfish

Rabbitfish

DID YOU KNOW?
Some electric rays can produce up to 1,000 volts to stun prey.

Eagle ray

Electric ray

Skate

Thornback ray

Monkfish

Stingray

© DIAGRAM

Most fishes today belong to a huge group called the teleosts. Each has a bony skeleton and fins that are held up by a series of thin rays.

RAY-FINNED FISHES have a long history that can be traced back 400 million years to a small fish, about 10 inches (25 cm) long, called *Cheirolepis*. This had a heavy skull, with bony plates on the cheeks, and thick, heavy scales. The fleshy part of the tail pointed upward, although this was balanced by a lower part held out by rays. The fish looks a little stiff and the side fins were not very maneuverable. However, similar large-eyed fish fossils are found all over the world. They were probably successful predators.

The story of ray-finned fish evolution is one of increasing maneuverability, a lightening of skeleton and scales, and increasing efficiency of gill-breathing. Some of this story can easily be seen in the fossil record, and various stages have been preserved to the present day by a small number of "primitive" living species.

The bichirs of Africa (10 species) have heavy scales, rather solid fins, and a row of finlets down the back. The young bichir has external gills like a tadpole. (Perhaps this was normal for early fishes.) The adult bichir has an air sac that allows it to breathe air if the

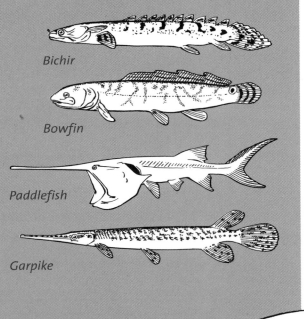

Bichir

Bowfin

Paddlefish

Garpike

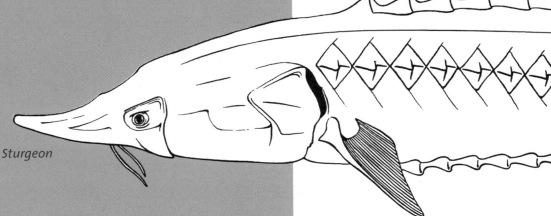

Sturgeon

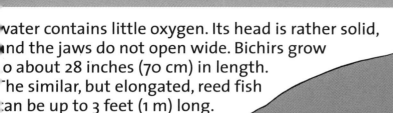

water contains little oxygen. Its head is rather solid, and the jaws do not open wide. Bichirs grow to about 28 inches (70 cm) in length. The similar, but elongated, reed fish can be up to 3 feet (1 m) long.

Sturgeons (27 species) have lost most of their bone, and have a cartilage skeleton and rather sharklike tail. There are rows of bony plates down their sides. They live in seas and fresh water. Some species make long migrations up rivers from the sea to spawn. Caviar comes from females, which each produce millions of eggs. Sturgeons swim near the bottom, feeding on mollusks, worms, and other small animals. The paddlefish of America and China are similar to sturgeons, but have mouths that open wide to catch plankton.

The bowfin (1 species) and garpike (7 species) live in North America. Fossils are found in other parts of the world. Bowfins grow to 3 feet (1 m) in length, whereas some garpike reach 8 feet (2.5 m). Both have primitive characteristics, such as thick scales, and can breathe air. They are predators.

Paddlefish
This fish swims with its mouth wide open, and the gills filter food from the water.

IT'S A FACT!
A sturgeon can live for over 100 years, and the biggest species grow to 20 feet (6 m) long, and weigh up to 1 ton (tonne).

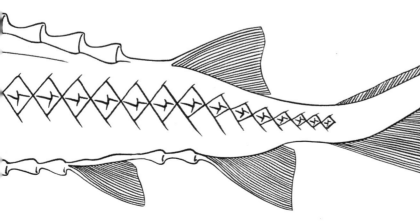

The teleosts are the most advanced group of ray-finned, bony fishes. The first fossils of this group existed more than 200 million years ago, but their huge success has come in the last 70 million years or so.

NOWADAYS there are about 20,000 species of teleosts spread through sea and freshwater habitats. As you might expect, they are enormously varied in shape, size, and habits, but they are all variations on a particularly successful body plan.

In teleosts the bones of the body support the fish in water, keep it in shape, and give something for the muscles to work on, but they are as light as they can be, and still provide the required strength. The bones of the head and jaws are particularly mobile, and many teleosts can instantly open their jaws very wide to trap prey. They are also good at using their mouths to create a current of water through the gills.

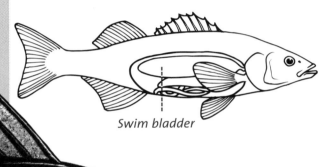

Swim bladder

Predators
John Dories have short, narrow, bodies, and capture prey by extending their voracious jaws.

Built for speed!
Marlins are fast swimmers, with highly developed streamlining, and powerful muscles.

In teleosts, the swim bladder is a balloon that can have its gas content precisely regulated to give the fish neutral buoyancy in the water. Because the fish is buoyant, the tail fin can be symmetrical above and below, to help drive the fish forward. (In other fish, an asymmetrical tail may be needed to provide lift as well as a forward push). Individual muscles move each fin ray. Fins, especially the pectoral and pelvic fins, can be turned in many directions. They are good brakes as well as being good for steering. On the outside, teleosts have light scales covered by a layer of enamel rather like that on human teeth. A single dorsal fin is normal.

A teleost fish may be able to hang in the water with little movement apart from its breathing, or may make use of its streamlined shape to make a sudden dart through the water to catch food, or escape an enemy. Some swim fast for long periods with comparatively little effort. Teleosts are very efficient swimming machines.

IT'S A FACT
The smallest teleost fish—and smallest adult vertebrate—is a Philippine goby which is 0.3 inches (0.75 cm) long, and weighs 0.00016 ounces (0.005 g). The ocean sunfish can weigh 1 ton (tonne).

Philippine goby

IT'S A FACT
Some fish, such as tuna, can reach very high speeds. For example, 45 miles per hour (72 kmph) has been recorded over a short distance.

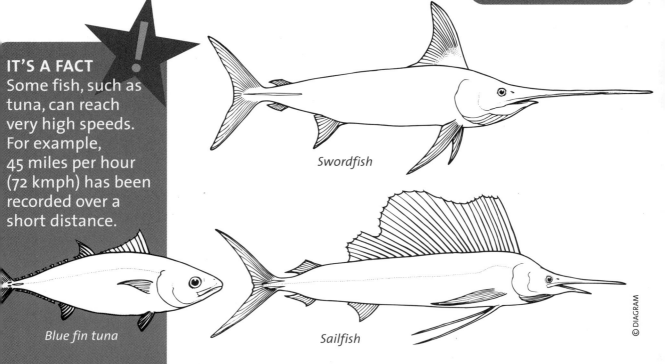

Swordfish

Blue fin tuna

Sailfish

© DIAGRAM

Seahorse

For some types of fish, a streamlined body is not needed. Fishes that live in confined spaces, for example among weeds or in the crevices of a coral reef, need to be able to steer precisely rather than to swim fast for any distance. Often such fish have thin, tall bodies, that are easy to turn quickly. They may swim mainly by rowing with their pectoral fins, or by rippling either their dorsal or anal fins instead.

THE ANGELFISH lives in weedy stretches of South American rivers. It can glide slowly and precisely through the water using its pectoral and dorsal fins, but a tail flick can produce a sudden turn of speed when darting at prey.

The marine butterfly fish has its mouth at the end of a long snout. It finds food by poking this snout into crevices in the coral. It needs to be able to position itself with precision, and has a high body and large pectoral fins for swimming.

A seahorse swims by rippling the dorsal fin in the middle of its back. It lives among weeds, and moves slowly in search of tiny prey that it sucks in through its tubular mouth. Instead of the usual tail fin, it has a prehensile tail that can hold on to weed.

DID YOU KNOW?
Garden eels live in colonies of burrows, which they rarely leave. Their shape makes it easy for them to dig.

A wrasse swims almost entirely by rowing with its pectoral fins. Wrasses pick at coral to find food. Some species specialize as cleaners of other fish, and need to maneuver carefully to pick parasites off their skin or gills.

Another method of dealing with tight spaces is to have a long, worm-like body to squeeze into burrows or rock crevices. Eels have this type of body. When they need to swim, they push on the water by throwing the body into curves with a wave of muscle contractions down its length, rather than relying on a tail fin.

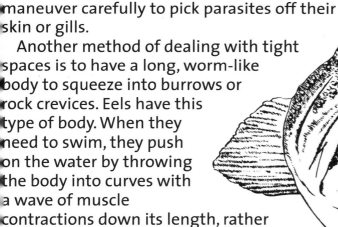

IT'S A FACT
Carapus fish spend much of their time inside sea urchins or other animals. The Mediterranean species reverses into the bodies of sea cucumbers. Its elongated body, and well-developed dorsal and ventral fins, allow it to wriggle in with ease.

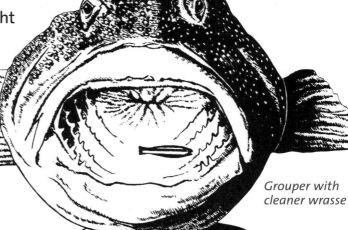

Grouper with cleaner wrasse

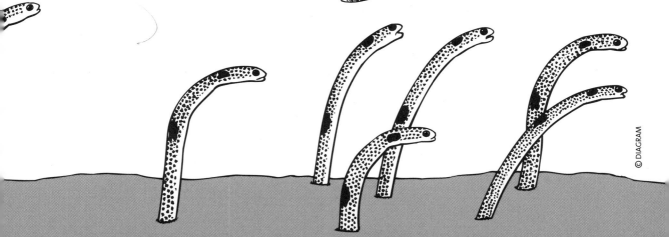

© DIAGRAM

Within the many kinds of teleost in the world today there are some amazing designs for living. There are even those which do very "unfishy" things like coming out of water and hopping around on mud (mudskippers), or even climbing trees (climbing perch).

THE FRESHWATER BUTTERFLY FISH can jump from water and flutter a short distance on "wings" made of pectoral fins. The flying fish of the sea can do better. They shoot out from the surface and glide for 330 feet (100 m) or more on their wide pectorals, sometimes, as they fall back, giving a kick with the tail to stay in the air for longer. They jump like this when predators chase them.

The sargassum fish, and the sea dragon—a relative of the seahorses—have amazing camouflage. Not only are they the right color to fit in with their seaweed surroundings, their shapes also match those of the weed they are hiding in.

Flatfish such as flounders and plaice have both eyes on one side of the head. One side of the body is white. The other is colored. They lie on the bottom, sometimes partially buried, and are beautifully camouflaged, especially as they can change color to some extent.

Other methods of protection include the sudden puffing up with air practiced by the puffer fishes. This turns these slow-swimming fishes into a spiny sphere that is difficult to eat.

Many fish have electric organs which can help them navigate. They are well developed in fishes

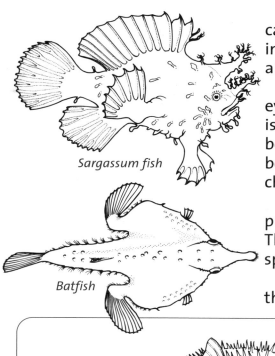

Sargassum fish

Batfish

Protection from attack
A pufferfish has a flexible, spiny skin. Whenever alarmed, it can enlarge into a prickly ball twice its normal size.

Holding on
Clingfish live in shallow water near shores, many of them located in the tropics. The pelvic fins are turned into efficient suckers.

uch as the electric eel and elephant-trunk mormyrids. These fish usually swim keeping their bodies straight to make this sense work best. Electric eels can also produce a discharge for protection.

Other modifications in teleosts include fins modified as suckers. The clingfish holds onto rocks at the edge of the sea by a sucker. The remora attaches itself by a modified dorsal fin to the underside of a shark or turtle and hitches a free ride.

Some fishes secrete venom. Weever fish and stonefish have venom spines in their dorsal fins. Dragonfish (*Pterois*) combine camouflage with poison spines on their fins.

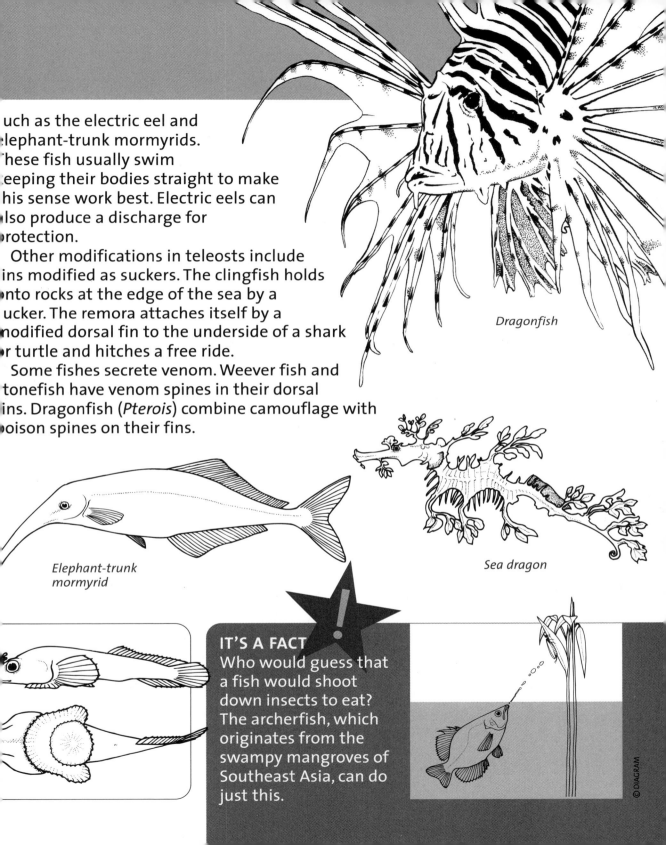

Dragonfish

Elephant-trunk mormyrid

Sea dragon

!

IT'S A FACT
Who would guess that a fish would shoot down insects to eat? The archerfish, which originates from the swampy mangroves of Southeast Asia, can do just this.

© DIAGRAM

Coelacanths are known from over 350 million years ago. They carried on through succeeding ages, but, from 200 million years ago, they gradually declined. The last fossil coelacanths are found in rocks about 70 million years old. Some scientists believed them to be extinct.

COELACANTHS are lobefinned fish. Unlike the teleosts, with fins supported by thin rays, the lobefins have bones at the base of the fins for support. In some lobefins the bones are arranged like the bones in our limbs. Most early coelacanths were small fish up to 10 inches (25 cm), long living in the sea. Some of the later ones were larger. Inside the fossil bodies a single "lung" can be seen, although it is armored with tiny scales. Presumably it could not be used for breathing, but what was its purpose? Most fish lay eggs, but a fossil coelacanth has been found with the skeleton of two babies inside. Some scientists suggested that this coelacanth produced live young. Others simply saw it as a cannibal.

In 1938 a living coelacanth was trawled up near the South African coast and shocked scientists. It was 5 feet (1.5 m) long, and weighed 180 pounds (80 kg). It was a massive bluish fish with the characteristic shape and lobefins of a coelacanth. Much could not be preserved for later investigation, but there was no doubt it was a coelacanth. Scientists wanted to find

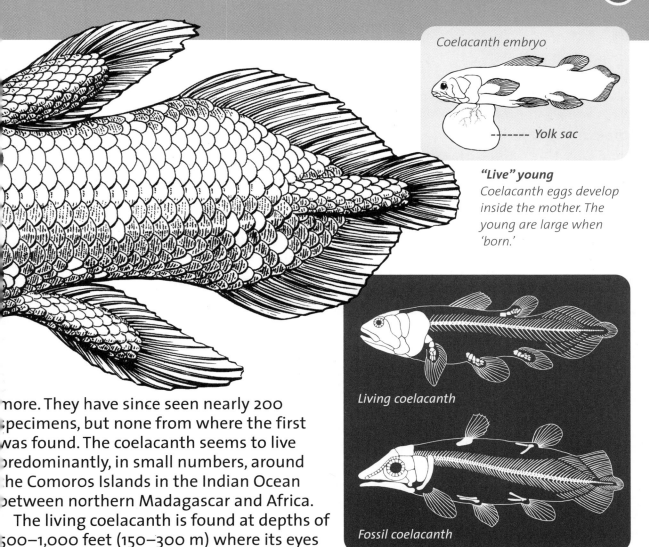

Coelacanth embryo

------- Yolk sac

"Live" young
Coelacanth eggs develop inside the mother. The young are large when 'born.'

Living coelacanth

Fossil coelacanth

Fossil evidence
The skeleton of the modern coelacanth is very similar to that of fossil coelacanths from nearly 200 million years ago.

more. They have since seen nearly 200 specimens, but none from where the first was found. The coelacanth seems to live predominantly, in small numbers, around the Comoros Islands in the Indian Ocean between northern Madagascar and Africa.

The living coelacanth is found at depths of 500–1,000 feet (150–300 m) where its eyes can operate in the very dim light. It is sluggish, remaining stationary in the water currents by using its highly mobile bony fins. It is a very oily fish, perhaps to provide buoyancy to counteract the weight of its bones, and its heavy bony scales. Its "lung" is actually full of oil, an adaptation to living its life at depths that were not necessarily usual for fossil coelacanths.

It feeds on a variety of small fishes and squids. A female coelacanth has been found carrying babies 12 inches (30 cm) long, showing that coelacanths can produce "live" young.

© DIAGRAM

Lungfish have a fossil ancestry tracing back 350 million years. Reasonably common as fossils, they declined in importance, and only three kinds of lungfish still live today.

THE AUSTRALIAN LUNGFISH is similar to a lungfish that lived 200 million years ago. It can breathe air, which is useful in poorly oxygenated water. The African lungfish is less like ancient forms, and the South American lungfish is long and eel-like. These fishes breathe air with their lungs, and can actually survive without water for some time. When water disappears in the dry season, they retreat into a cocoon made of mucus and wait for its return. Typical lungfish fins were lobed and bony, but these are much reduced in the living African and South American forms.

Lungfish can breathe air and have limb-like legs, but it appears that they never colonized the land. The coelacanths and lungfishes evolved from primitive lobe-finned fish ancestors, as did other groups of early fishes. From one of them the first four-legged creatures (tetrapods) evolved. Most scientists agree on this, but have long argued over exactly which fishes these tetrapods' ancestors were.

The forerunners of tetrapods would have breathed air through nostrils that opened into the mouth, and had lobed fins with a bony skeleton. *Eusthenopteron* is one fish that has been thought a possible ancestor. *Panderichthys* is another more recent favorite.

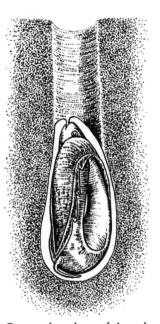

Burrowing down (above)
The African lungfish can survive several years of drought cocooned in a burrow, but burns up body muscle.

Ichthyostega
An early amphibian, this creature had legs with toes, but also tail fin rays like a fish.

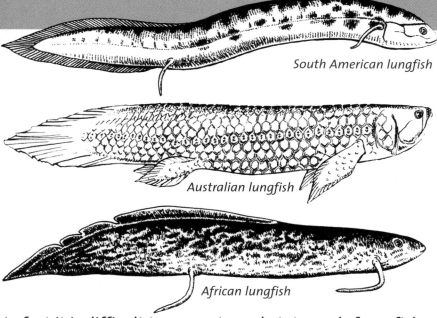

South American lungfish

Australian lungfish

African lungfish

Lungfish (left)
For hundreds of millions of years, lungfish were found all over the world, but now they only survive in three southern continents.

In fact it is difficult to separate early tetrapods from fishes. Many still had tail fins, and fishlike skulls. On the other hand, early tetrapods had recognizable legs, although they sometimes had eight, seven, or six toes, rather than the five that later became standard. They had a ribcage to support the lungs. Shallow, warm, fresh waters and swamps provided a home where being able to swim, and also being able to walk or slither on land, could both be important.

Between 400 and 350 million years ago fish had given rise to the tetrapods we would call "amphibians" and, for 80 million years after that, these were the dominant animals on land. Some grew 13 feet (4 m) long or more and were fearsome predators.

The great variety of these amphibians went into decline once reptiles evolved. One group left descendants in the amphibians we have today, but few reach anything like the size and physical dominance of their ancient relatives.

Eusthenopteron
This creature could probably breathe air, and had paired fins with bones arranged rather like those in human legs. It may have been able to cross short distances of mud between ponds.

© DIAGRAM

Although the tetrapods' great leap forward was to conquer land, many early "amphibians" stayed in the water or returned to live there. Many had legs too small to support their weight on land. Some were large and heavy, perhaps crocodile-like in habits, moving through the swamps in search of prey. Others were fish-shaped, sometimes elongated like an eel. Yet others were quite bizarre shapes.

CYCLOTOSAURUS was a large "amphibian" with a long head like a crocodile, and pointed teeth for catching fish. Although it grew to over 13 feet (4 m), its legs were comparatively small, and it spent most of its time in the water. The small *Sauropleura*, about 8 inches (20 cm) long, had much reduced legs, and a body like a stretched-out salamander. Even longer were *Ophiderpeton* at 30 inches (75 cm) and *Dolichosoma*, types in which the number of bones in the backbone was greatly increased. They must have looked like snakes as they swam and wriggled through the swamps.

Diplocaulus was an "amphibian" with a flattened skull that stretched into "horns" at the sides. As the animal grew to its maximum 2 feet (60 cm) these horns grew proportionately bigger. The small mouth was just under the front of the head. *Gerrothorax* was another oddity. It retained gills as an adult, so it still looked like a tadpole with little legs, even though it grew to 3 feet (1 m) long. Both these animals were aquatic.

Covering the options

The Axolotl lives in water, despite its legs, and keeps some larval characteristics throughout its life.

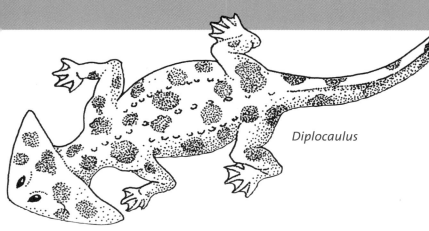

Diplocaulus

Some modern amphibians, like their ancestors, have given up land living and become totally aquatic. The Mexican *Axolotl* develops legs but retains gills all its life, and reproduces as a "giant larva." The proteid salamanders, including the olm of the Balkans, and the mudpuppies of America, are totally aquatic, with well-developed gills and very small legs. The olm lives in underground caves, is sightless, and has no skin pigment.

Sirens are another family of aquatic North American salamanders. The greater siren, at 3 feet (90 cm) long one of the biggest living amphibians, has a long body, external gills, tiny front legs, and no back legs.

Living on the land
A land-living "amphibian" from over 250 million years ago, Cacops *was just 16 inches (40 cm) long.*

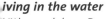

Living in the water
With weak legs, Paracyclotosaurus, *from 210 million years ago, probably spent its life in water. It grew to 8 feet (2.25 m) long.*

© DIAGRAM

Prehistoric swimming reptiles

Reptiles were the first backboned animals to lay shelled eggs, and have a dry, scaly, waterproof skin. They are no longer restricted to water. Many are good at living in dry conditions, even in deserts. However, throughout their history, many groups of reptiles have returned to the sea or fresh water, and have become adapted to a completely aquatic life.

THE FIRST REPTILES to take to the water were the mesosaurs, nearly 300 million years ago. They had long flat tails that helped to propel them through the water. The hind legs were also large and powerful. They grew up to 3 feet (1 m) long, and had long jaws and many pointed, interlocking teeth which may have been good for catching fish, although some people believe they strained small creatures from the water. Mesosaurs lived in fresh water.

Placodonts ate mollusks. They had enormous flat teeth in their jaws to crush their food, and peglike teeth at the front to gather it. They swam with long flattened tails and webbed feet, but had a tubby body. Placodonts lived between 250 and 206 million years ago. Nothosaurs lived about 225 million years ago. They grew up to 13 feet (4 m) long, but many were smaller. The tail could be used for swimming, and the legs may have worked as paddles, though they were not particularly suited for this. Common some 80 million years ago, mosasaurs were ocean-going lizards that swam using their long powerful tails. They had long skulls with jaws containing many big curved teeth. They could have caught very large

WAY BACK IN TIME?
Placodus, dating from about 220 million years ago, was 6 feet (2 m) long, and probably swam slowly. It gathered mollusks with its peg-like front teeth.

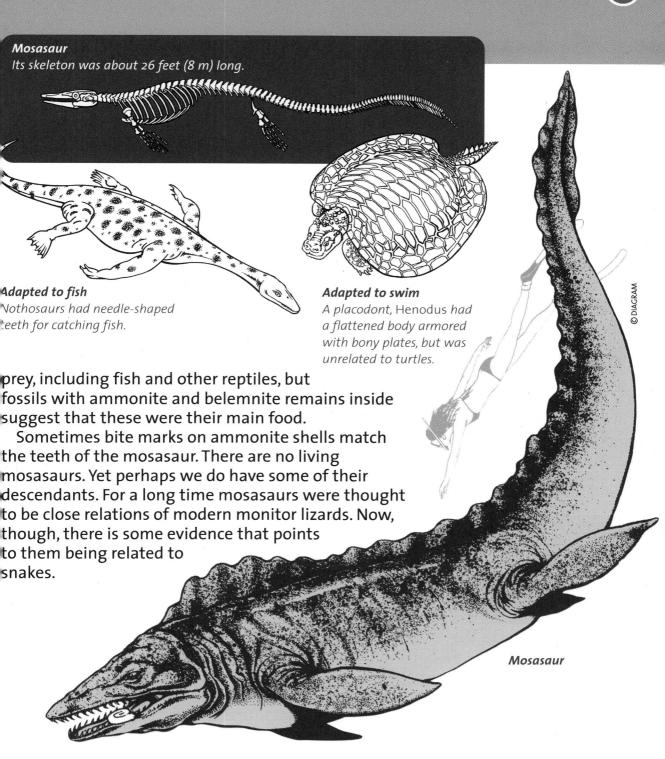

Mosasaur
Its skeleton was about 26 feet (8 m) long.

Adapted to fish
Nothosaurs had needle-shaped teeth for catching fish.

Adapted to swim
A placodont, Henodus had a flattened body armored with bony plates, but was unrelated to turtles.

© DIAGRAM

prey, including fish and other reptiles, but fossils with ammonite and belemnite remains inside suggest that these were their main food.

Sometimes bite marks on ammonite shells match the teeth of the mosasaur. There are no living mosasaurs. Yet perhaps we do have some of their descendants. For a long time mosasaurs were thought to be close relations of modern monitor lizards. Now, though, there is some evidence that points to them being related to snakes.

Mosasaur

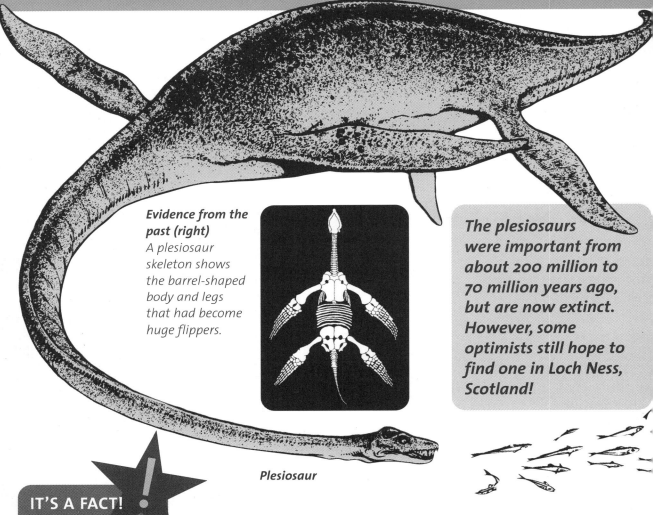

Evidence from the past (right)
A plesiosaur skeleton shows the barrel-shaped body and legs that had become huge flippers.

Plesiosaur

The plesiosaurs were important from about 200 million to 70 million years ago, but are now extinct. However, some optimists still hope to find one in Loch Ness, Scotland!

IT'S A FACT!
Elasmosaurus, a plesiosaur, grew to 40 feet (12 m) or more in length, but more than half of this length was its neck. Inside the neck were 76 vertebrae.

PLESIOSAURS probably developed from the nothosaurs, but became better adapted for swimming. With a broad, flat body and a short tail, plesiosaurs relied on their legs for propulsion. All four were turned into large flippers. These were flexible and could lift as well as push the animal forward, as it 'flew' through the water.

There were two main trends in the plesiosaurs. Some developed long necks, while others kept them short. The short-necked plesiosaurs are sometimes given a different name—pliosaurs.

Long-necked plesiosaurs had relatively small heads equipped with sharp teeth. We can imagine these fish-eaters making a sudden sideways grab for prey using their flexible necks. Perhaps, too, they could rest at the surface and lower the head to peer into the depths. These were air-breathers like other reptiles and, when active, they would have to return to the surface regularly to breathe. It is not known how they reproduced but, although well adapted for swimming, their limbs might still have moved them clumsily on land, like a modern sea turtle. They may have come ashore to lay eggs.

The pliosaurs, with short necks, had a more streamlined appearance. They still rowed with paddle-shaped limbs, a swimming method similar to that of modern sea lions. They had comparatively large heads with strong teeth and jaws. They probably chased and caught large prey, including a variety of fish and other marine reptiles.

Although there were small kinds of plesiosaur, no longer than 6 feet (2 m) or so, many were big animals with a length of 13 feet (4 m) or more, and some were giants over 40 feet (12 m) long. There must have been plenty of food in the ancient seas to fuel these animals.

IT'S A FACT!
For years *Kronosaurus* was thought to have been the biggest pliosaur. At up to 55 feet (17 m) in length, with one quarter taken up by its huge head, this creature was a ferocious predator. Fossil neck bones of another pliosaur, which may have reached 65 feet (20 m) long, and weighed 50 tons (tonnes), were found in 2002.

Pliosaur

Some of the best-adapted swimmers ever to live in the sea were known as ichthyosaurs. They were reptiles, not fishes or dolphins. Ichthyosaurs lived from 250 until 90 million years ago.

IT'S A FACT
The ichthyosaurs are among the animals with the biggest eyes. One, *Ophthalmosaurus*, probably had the biggest eyes in relation to its size of any animal. They helped the creature to gather light well when it dived into the depths.

THE EARLIEST ICHTHYOSAURS had long bodies and tails, but they soon evolved into a typical "fish" shape, with a large head smoothly joined to a streamlined body. There were four limbs, with the back pair smaller. All had broad-based "fins," flexible enough to help with steering, but not to paddle the animal along. The bones within corresponded to those in human limbs, but were much shorter.

The number of round bones in each finger was increased. Sometimes the number of fingers was more or less than the standard five.

An ichthyosaur flexed its body to drive the tail from side to side to push on the water. Some fossils show the outline of the soft parts of their bodies as well as the bones, so we know the shape of the large tails.

Living like dolphins
Ichthyosaurs pursued fish and ammonites through the Mesozoic seas. Although reptiles, not mammals, they possibly existed in dolphin-like groups.

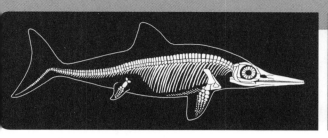

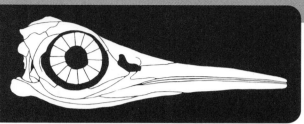

The backbone bent downwards into the lower lobe of the tail. A large dorsal fin acted as a stabilizer.

Most ichthyosaurs had long jaws with many pointed teeth, and caught prey such as fish and ammonites. The eyes were often very large so they must have hunted by sight. A strong ring of bones supported each eye, keeping it in shape as it swam. Nostrils were set well back from the front of the snout, at the top of the head near the eyes. These were air-breathing animals, like any reptile, and would have come to the surface regularly. The single ear bone connecting the eardrum to the middle ear was massive in ichthyosaurs, unlike that in most reptiles. Sounds, which travel well in water, were important to them, as they are to whales.

Ichthyosaurs were so well adapted for the sea that it is surprising that they became extinct before the less streamlined plesiosaurs. We do not know why.

Temnodontosaurus
This large ichthyosaur grew to 30 feet (9 m) or more in length.

Fossil evidence
The down-turned tail bones, and huge bones supporting the eye, are typical of ichthyosaurs.

DO YOU KNOW?
How did ichthyosaurs breed? They could not have moved on land, or laid eggs there like most reptiles. Ichthyosaurs bore their young alive. Some fossils show babies inside the mother. One fossil may be an ichthyosaur that died while giving birth. A baby appears to be emerging from the mother's body tail-first, as dolphins do today.

The first turtles known are fossils over 200 million years old. They had shells and horny beaks, much like those of modern tortoises and turtles, but still had some teeth in the roof of the mouth. Later turtles lost these. These first turtles could not pull their heads into their shells.

IN TORTOISES AND TURTLES the outside shell is made up of horny plates. Underneath are bony plates fused to one another and to the backbone and ribs, the whole making a solid, rigid box. Although this design has some disadvantages, the protection it gives has allowed it to survive almost unchanged for 200 million years.

The earliest turtles lived in freshwater swamps. Later some became land tortoises, and others became adapted for a totally aquatic life in the sea. Most, though, remain as freshwater terrapins and turtles, living in, and around, water. Typically they have webbed feet and flattened shells, and are good, but not especially fast, swimmers. They feed on slow-moving small prey such as worms and insect larvae, although some also eat plants. All turtles need to breathe air but, as they are cold-blooded, use little energy if they are not active, so may stay underwater for minutes or even hours.

IT'S A FACT
Although many small freshwater turtles only lay a handful of eggs, the green sea turtle lays clutches of up to 100. In some parts of the world a female will lay up to 11 clutches in a year. This compensates for the tremendous losses suffered due to predation on eggs and baby turtles.

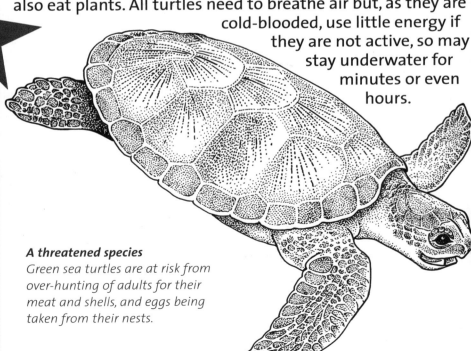

A threatened species
Green sea turtles are at risk from over-hunting of adults for their meat and shells, and eggs being taken from their nests.

Sea turtles stay in the sea for most of their lives. Their shells are lightened by the reduction of bone in the shell to a series of struts, but the horny plates on the outside remain, except in the largest living sea turtle, the leatherback, which can weigh 1,500 pounds (680 kg). Sea turtles can swim at speeds up to 20 miles per hour (30 kmph) on occasion—faster than humans can run—but usually travel more slowly. The long, front flippers row the turtle through the water. The back feet act as rudders. Most sea turtles feed on small animals, although adult green turtles eat sea grasses near the shore.

All turtles lay typical, reptile-shelled eggs. These must be laid on land, so terrapins lay them in earth on river banks. However, a female sea turtle has to drag herself out of the sea to scrape a nest hole in the sand.

IT'S A FACT

The incubation temperature of loggerhead turtle eggs affects whether hatchlings will be male or female. At 85°F (30°C) the numbers are equal, but at four degrees Fahrenheit (2°C) above this temperature, only females are produced, and four degrees Fahrenheit (2°C) below it, only males are born.

Leatherback turtles
These roam warm and cool oceans, and can dive to a depth of 3,000 feet (1,000 m).

Shell structure

Scutes
Carapace
Rib fused to carapace
Vertebrae fused to carapace
Plastron

Neck vertebrae
Pectoral girdle
Pelvic girdle

© DIAGRAM

Crocodiles

Crocodilians, the largest living reptile group that includes crocodiles, alligators, and gavials, were successful in the time of the dinosaurs. In the last 65 million years their design has hardly changed.

MOST CROCODILES AND ALLIGATORS spend their lives in and around water, where their adaptations come into their own. The long, heavily-muscled tail has flat sides. It is used to propel the animal forward. The legs are often folded by the sides as a crocodile swims. The eyes are on top of the head. The nostrils are on a bump at the tip of the snout. A crocodile can submerge with only its eyes and nose above water, allowing it to breathe while keeping watch for prey coming to the waterside.

Crocodiles are unusual among reptiles. They have a bony palate from the tip of the snout to the back of the mouth, separating the mouth cavity from the nose.

Deinosuchus (below)
A modern crocodile (below left) is compared with Deinosuchus, which had a skull 6 feet (2 m) long, and grew up to 33 feet (10 m) long.

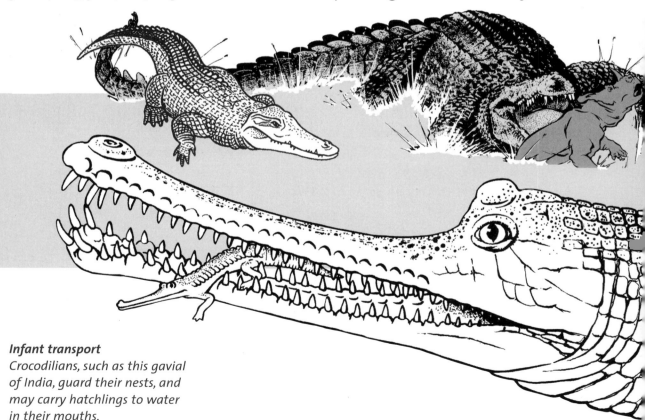

Infant transport
Crocodilians, such as this gavial of India, guard their nests, and may carry hatchlings to water in their mouths.

A flap of skin can close off the back of the mouth. A crocodile can breathe with its mouth open underwater as it catches prey. This feature is fully developed only in "modern" crocodiles of the last 65 million years.

Crocodilians with narrow snouts, such as the gavial of India, are specialist fish-eaters. Those with broad snouts may take anything that they are able to overpower. There are some 22 living species of crocodile and alligator. They range in size from about 4 feet (1.2 m) long up to 20 feet (6 m) or more for the saltwater crocodile, which is found around coasts and estuaries from India to Australia. It sometimes swims across the open sea.

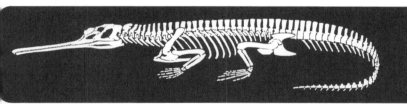

Mystriosuchus *skeleton (above)*
This was not a crocodile, but a phytosaur. Phytosaurs were common over 200 million years ago.

IT'S A FACT

There were sea crocodiles 150 million years ago, but they were not closely related to those existing today. *Metriorhynchus* was not armored with bony plates like present-day crocodiles, but had a fish-like tail fin and limbs modified as paddles. In some ways it was better suited to swimming than modern crocodilians. The phytosaurs were forerunners of the crocodiles over 200 million years ago, with a similar appearance and probably similar habits, though they were only distant relations, not crocodile ancestors. Long jaws contained many sharp teeth, and they were probably fish-eaters. Interestingly, their nostrils were right on top of the head, near their eyes.

© DIAGRAM

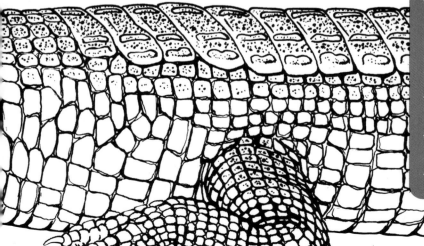

Although most snakes live on land, there are about 60 species that are adapted to life in the sea.

THE SEA SNAKES are related to cobras and, like them, have powerful venom that acts on the nervous system of their prey. Some sea snakes have the most powerful venom of all snakes. They need to subdue prey quickly so it does not escape into the vast ocean. Most have quite short fangs, and take small prey, including fish and invertebrates. Some species specialize in eels, which are an ideal shape for a sea snake to swallow. They rarely bite humans.

Sea snakes are mostly found in the seas of southeast Asia and the western Pacific, although one species, the black-and-yellow sea snake, is found in waters extending from the eastern Pacific to the Indian Ocean. Most are coastal animals, but the black-and-yellow sea snake lives in the open sea.

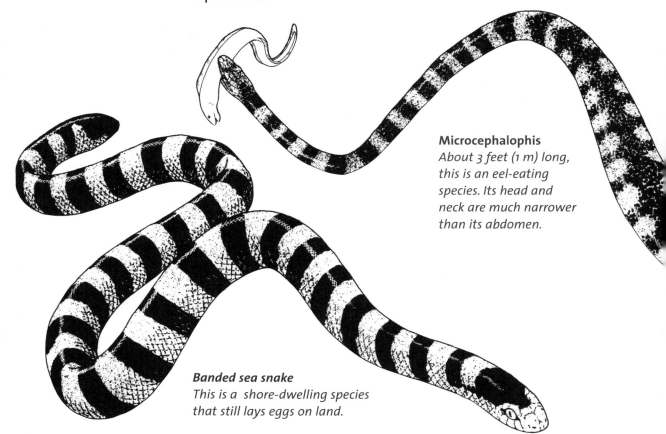

Microcephalophis
About 3 feet (1 m) long, this is an eel-eating species. Its head and neck are much narrower than its abdomen.

Banded sea snake
This is a shore-dwelling species that still lays eggs on land.

Sea snakes are adapted for swimming by having flat tails to push on the water. They have large lungs which extend along almost the entire length of the body. These give them buoyancy, making swimming easier, and also contain plenty of air. Sea snakes may stay under water for two hours.

On top of the snout sea snakes have nostrils that can be closed with a valve to keep water out. Land snakes usually have large scales on the belly to grip the ground. The only sea snakes with these are a few that lay eggs on the shore. Most sea snakes have small belly scales and never come to land. They produce half-a-dozen living young, rather than lay eggs.

IT'S A FACT
Although only about two percent of modern snake species live in the sea, some scientists think that snakes evolved there. A fossil called *Pachyrhachis* lived in shallow seas about 100 million years ago. Although it had tiny hind limbs, its skull is snakelike, with wide-opening jaws. It seems as if snakes were living in the sea at the dawn of their history. A case can be made for snakes having evolved in the sea from the same group as the giant sea-going lizards, the mosasaurs. This does not mean that present-day sea snakes are primitive. They belong to an advanced family of snakes, and their ancestors spent time on land.

Black-and-yellow sea snake (right)
Spending its life in the ocean, this species hunts fish by stealth rather than pursuit.

© DIAGRAM

Mammals are well adapted for living on land, but several groups, most notably whales, have evolved an aquatic lifestyle.

WHALES ARE STREAMLINED, even though some are massive. The neck is short, and the head joins the body smoothly. The forelimbs have turned into flippers, which help to lift the front end of the animal when swimming. The hind limbs have disappeared, except for the remnants of hip bones hidden within the body. Propulsion is provided by the tail, which has flukes made largely of gristle; these extend horizontally, unlike a fish's vertical tail. Muscles move the rear of the body up and down to work the flukes. Whales' land ancestry is obvious here, as an up-and-down movement of the back is used by running mammals such as cheetahs.

The head and jaws are large. Jaws are adapted to the different ways of feeding of various types of whale. The nostrils have shifted to the top of the head where they form a blowhole, which is normally closed, except when taking a breath. The ear-flaps characteristic of mammals have disappeared, and the ear entrance is tiny, but the internal ear is highly developed and hearing is a very important sense. Another mammal characteristic, a coat of fur, has also disappeared in the whale group, although some have a few bristles that may have a sensory function. The bare skin is structured to help smooth the flow of water across it. Underneath there is a thick layer of fat—the blubber—that gives insulation in water.

Basilosaurus
This early whale had an elongated body and serrated teeth for catching fish.

Although not necessarily all direct ancestors, fossils of primitive whales give a good idea of the stages that mammals went through in their evolution to modern whales.

Whales and cattle both come from a mammal with five toes that each ended in a hoof. Unlike today's hoofed mammals, it probably ate meat. *Ambulocetus* was an early "whale," but had large paddle-like limbs, and could still move on land. *Protocetus* was about 10 feet (3 m) long, and a good swimmer. As early whales developed the tail as the main means of propulsion, the hind limbs disappeared. Whales became completely aquatic. Some grew to enormous sizes, like the 60 feet (18 m) long *Basilosaurus*.

IT'S A FACT
Breathing is quite explosive in many whales, and 90 percent of the contents of their lungs may be changed at each breath, much more than in land mammals.

Early whales

Ambulocetus

Protocetus

Fin whale skull

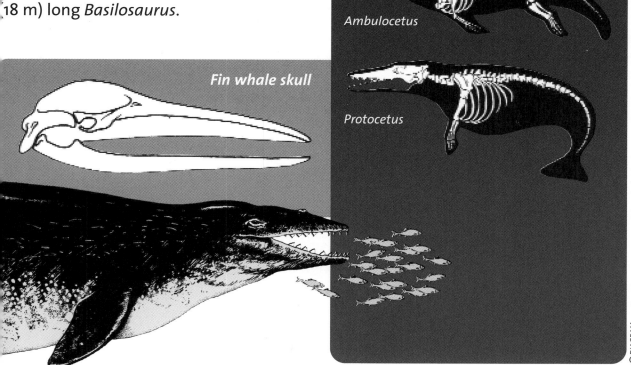

© DIAGRAM

Of the whale species in the world, 66 out of 76 belong to the toothed group. Many are not very big—dolphins or porpoises—but the toothed whales also include the biggest predators on the planet.

Melon

Acoustic focusing
The prominent "melon" forehead of dolphins focuses the echolocating sounds they produce.

THE BIGGEST TOOTHED WHALE is the great sperm whale. Males are commonly 50 feet (15 m) long and can grow to 65 feet (20 m). Females are smaller. Sperm whales can weigh 36 tons (tonnes) or more. Even a newborn baby is 13 feet (4 m) long and weighs a ton (tonne).

Toothed whales typically have a row of similarly shaped teeth along the jaw. They are suitable for catching fish or squid, and as in adult humans, the one set of teeth must last a lifetime. In long-beaked dolphins there can be as many as 260 teeth. At the other extreme, the narwhal has a single tooth which protrudes as a spiral tusk. Unlike all other mammals, toothed whales have just a single nostril, the two nasal passages joining before reaching the outside of the head. The jaw is long, and in most toothed whales the skull is asymmetrical. In front of the skull is the "melon," the rounded "forehead" seen in dolphins and others. It contains a

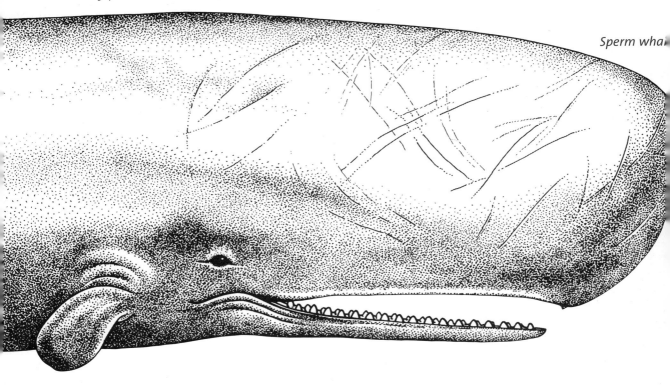

Sperm wha

waxy lens-shaped organ, which is believed to focus sounds produced in the nose behind and beam them forward.

Echoes return from objects in front of the animal and travel through oil-filled sinuses in the lower jaw to reach the inner ear. The echoes allow the animal to navigate and discover a lot about its surroundings without using its eyes. Useful in the sea, this sense is even more vital to river dolphins that live in muddy water in some of the world's largest rivers, and are virtually blind.

The sperm whale catches fish and squid, diving into the depths as much as 6,500 feet (2,000 m) down to find prey. Sometimes it tackles giant squid, but it mostly eats squid about 3 feet (1 m) long. A sperm whale may dive for as long as one hour, replenishing its air supply with 30 or more huge breaths when it returns to the surface. Whales do not have big lungs, but they can store oxygen in their muscles attached to a pigment called myoglobin, and this helps prolong their air supply. Smaller whales and dolphins do not dive for so long, but can remain under for minutes at a time.

IT'S A FACT
In spite of their size, whales are difficult to study in the wild. The beaked whales, a family of 18 species ranging from 16 feet (5 m) to 32 feet (10 m) long, manage to remain largely undetected in the ocean depths. Only a tiny number of chance strandings have allowed scientists to see and name some of the species.

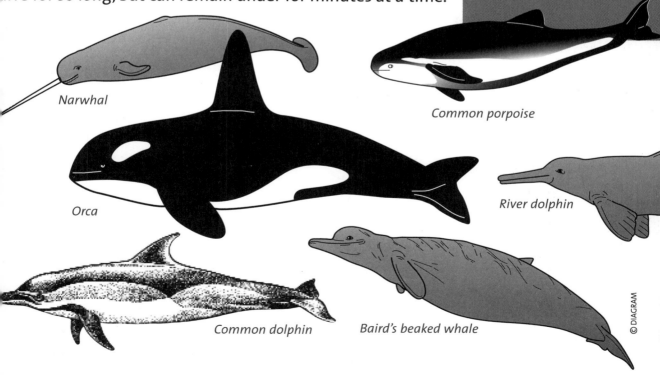

Narwhal

Common porpoise

Orca

River dolphin

Common dolphin

Baird's beaked whale

© DIAGRAM

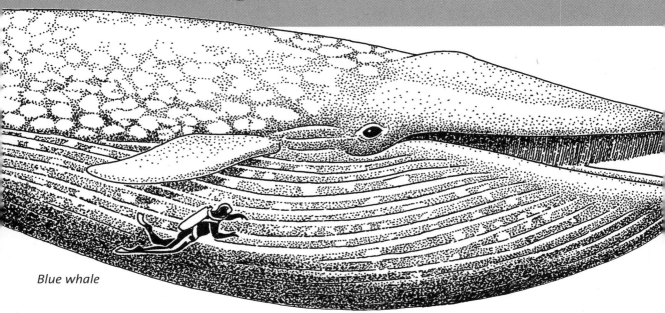

Blue whale

The biggest of all whales feeds simply on tiny food.

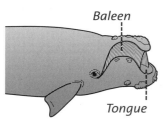

Baleen

Tongue

Catching their prey
The horny plates of baleen hang from the upper jaw of the whale, making a giant sieve for trapping krill.

THE BLUE WHALE, probably the biggest animal that has ever lived, feeds on the small crustaceans, krill. It does this by filtering them out of the seawater using plates of baleen, or "whalebone," inside its mouth. These are not bone at all but are made of keratin, as is hair. Baleen plates grow from the gums and palate at the sides of the mouth, and take the place of teeth, which are present in embryo baleen whales but never in adults. Smooth at the outer edge, the baleen plates fray into a fringe of threads on the sides facing the tongue. The whale swims with its mouth open, and thousands of krill are trapped in the threads. As the mouth closes, the huge tongue then scrapes them off and sends them down the throat. The tongue of a blue whale can weigh four tons (tonnes). The baleen keeps growing throughout a whale's life. This makes up for the fringe wearing away in use.

There are ten species of whale that have baleen plates. They have probably evolved from toothed whales, and fossils have been found with widely-spaced teeth, and the beginnings of baleen whale characteristics.

The head and mouth of baleen whales are huge compared to the body, usually up to 40 percent of the total length in the

owhead whale. Different species have baleen of different
ngths. Right whales and bowheads have high arching jaws to
:commodate their long baleen. The two halves of the lower
w, freed from the need to bite hard, are only loosely
onnected at the front. Different lengths of baleen, different
umbers of plates, and differences in the fineness of the
inge, provide filters adapted for different types of food.
Some baleen whales mainly eat krill, others tiny copepods,
d others feed largely on fish.

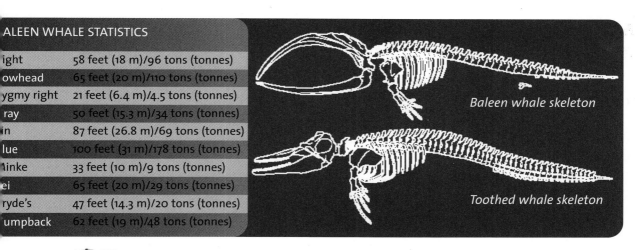

ALEEN WHALE STATISTICS	
ight	58 feet (18 m)/96 tons (tonnes)
owhead	65 feet (20 m)/110 tons (tonnes)
ygmy right	21 feet (6.4 m)/4.5 tons (tonnes)
ray	50 feet (15.3 m)/34 tons (tonnes)
in	87 feet (26.8 m)/69 tons (tonnes)
lue	100 feet (31 m)/178 tons (tonnes)
Minke	33 feet (10 m)/9 tons (tonnes)
ei	65 feet (20 m)/29 tons (tonnes)
ryde's	47 feet (14.3 m)/20 tons (tonnes)
umpback	62 feet (19 m)/48 tons (tonnes)

Baleen whale skeleton

Toothed whale skeleton

© DIAGRAM

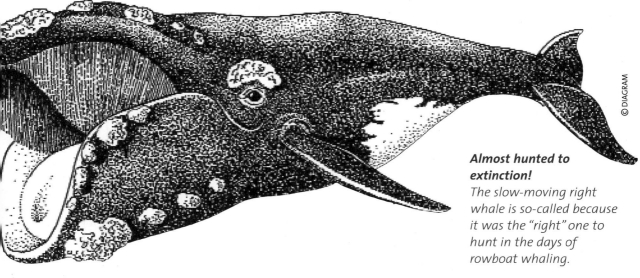

Almost hunted to extinction!
The slow-moving right whale is so-called because it was the "right" one to hunt in the days of rowboat whaling.

Present-day hoofed mammals all belong to one of two groups: one contains even-toed hoofed mammals, such as deer, giraffe, and antelope; the other odd-toed hoofed mammals, such as horses, and rhinoceroses.

HOOFED MAMMALS are essentially built as runners, but the heaviest of all the even-toed hoofed mammals, the hippopotamus spends much of its time in the water. Weighing up to three tons (tonnes) with rather short legs, the hippo is not elegant on land. With its weight supported by water however, it can move with agility—either running and springing on the bottom, or swimming.

Hippos spend most of the day in the water, but come on land at night to graze. They have bare skins like other large mammals, with a layer of fat beneath for insulation in water. The eyes protrude from the top of the head, the nostrils are on a bump on the snout, and the ear-flaps are small. Ears and nostrils can be closed when hippos dive. They are able to rest with just nose and eyes above water.

In a warm period between Ice Ages 120,000 years

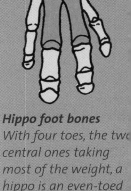

Hippo foot bones
With four toes, the two central ones taking most of the weight, a hippo is an even-toed hoofed mammal.

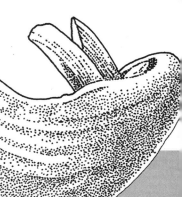

IT'S A FACT
Another group of strange amphibious mammals lived some 20 million years ago. The desmostylids lived around the edge of the Pacific. Clumsy-looking, with a crouching stance and stout limbs, these animals had forward-pointing tusks. Their exact way of life can only be guessed. In the past, both mollusk-eating and plant-eating diets have been suggested for them, but some form of plant-eating seems most likely. Their strange cheek teeth were columnar, and grew forward during life like those of elephants and sea cows, probably the closest living relations of the desmostylids. They died out completely. There are no living mammals remotely comparable.

go, hippos lived in Britain. onger ago still, slightly more primitive ypes lived in India. Now hippos are onfined to Africa, with the smaller, less quatic, pygmy hippo only to be found in orests in West Africa.

There are no fossils that show the mmediate ancestors of hippos, although cientists link them to pigs. A group of large mammals alled anthracotheres, also on the pig side of the even-oed, hoofed animal family tree, flourished some 20 nillion years ago. The beds in which the fossils are ound suggest that anthracotheres were also mphibious. They may have had an ancestor in ommon with hippos.

Anthracothere, hippo, and pygmy hippo
A comparison of sizes between the two modern amphibious, hoofed mammals, and an ancient, piglike anthracothere.

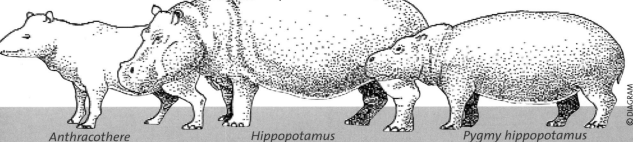

Anthracothere   *Hippopotamus*   *Pygmy hippopotamus*

© DIAGRAM

Unlike other sea mammals, dugongs and manatees are plant eaters, hence their alternative name of sea cows. Large—up to 15 feet (4.6 m), and 1.6 tons (tonnes) in weight—they are usually slow-moving, and graze on beds of sea grass near the coasts of tropical and subtropical seas. Their bodies work less than a quarter as fast as those of humans, and lose heat rapidly in water below 70°F (20°C), even with fat under the skin and around some body organs, so they do not live in cooler waters.

S TELLER'S SEA COW was the biggest of a line of sea cows whose fossils can be traced back over 60 million years. During that time the hind limbs disappeared, and the head and jaws became more specialized. The lips, with bristles both inside and out, are mobile, and pull vegetation into the jaws. The food is then mashed by either horny plates (in dugongs) or by teeth (in manatees).

A further difference between manatees and dugongs is that manatees have rounded tails and dugongs have tails shaped like the tail flukes of whales.

In both, powerful muscles extend along the belly and help them swim. The front limbs form paddles that help to steer, and can also push food toward the mouth. The eyes are small and poor. There are no earflaps and the external ear opening is tiny, but sea cows have good hearing. The part of the brain used for the sense of smell is large, although, as sea cows usually have their nostrils closed, it is not certain how much they use this sense. The brain of a sea cow looks simple compared to many mammals. The intestines are very long and adapted for the plant diet. The bones are very dense. Manatees have six neck bones, unlike the seven in almost all other mammals. The dugong lives in coastal waters from

Dugong

Manatee

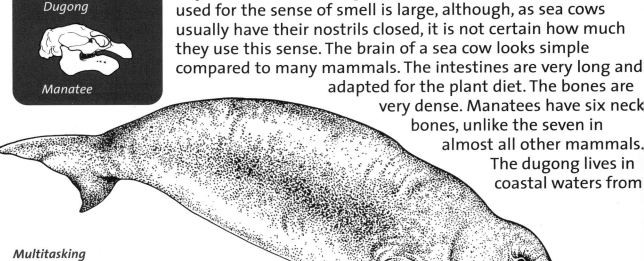

Multitasking
While a dugong grazes on the seabed, it also "walks" on its flippers.

East Africa across to Australia and the southwest Pacific, although it is now absent, or much reduced, in many places due to hunting for meat, oil, and skins.

There are three species of manatee: one lives on the coasts of West Africa; another, the largest, in the area from Florida and the Caribbean down to Brazil. The third is confined to the fresh waters of the Amazon basin. They too have been over-hunted, but are now actively conserved in some places.

IT'S A FACT
The only sea cow known to live in cold water was Steller's sea cow. A party of shipwrecked Russian explorers discovered it in 1741. It lived on the shores of two subarctic islands, and probably numbered only a few thousand. It was huge, up to 26 feet (8 m) long and nearly 6 tons (tonnes) in weight, and fed on the beds of kelp seaweed. It was good to eat and easy to catch, and by 1768 it was extinct. Fossils of the species from 100,000 years ago occur from Japan to California.

Manatee (right)
The cheek teeth, like those of an elephant, are replaced from the back of the jaw as the old ones wear down.

Ancestor (below)
Halitherium, a sea cow dating from about 25 million years ago, was already similar to modern dugongs.

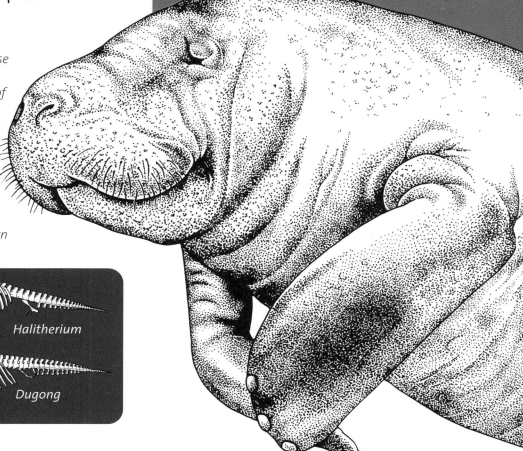

Halitherium

Dugong

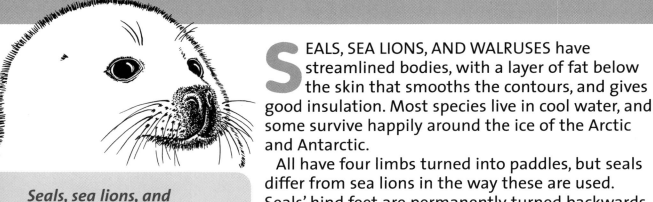

SEALS, SEA LIONS, AND WALRUSES have streamlined bodies, with a layer of fat below the skin that smooths the contours, and gives good insulation. Most species live in cool water, and some survive happily around the ice of the Arctic and Antarctic.

All have four limbs turned into paddles, but seals differ from sea lions in the way these are used. Seals' hind feet are permanently turned backwards and used rather like a double fish tail, sculling them from side to side for propulsion. The front flippers are either used to steer, or are held to the side. In sea lions and walruses, the front flippers are larger, and they are used to row the animal through the water, the rear flippers acting as a rudder. Their rear flippers can turn under the body for walking.

The pinnipeds have evolved from land carnivores, and shared an ancestor, a long time ago, with bears. The earliest stages in their evolution are not known from fossils, but there are fossils from the last 25 million years,

Seals, sea lions, and walruses—collectively known as pinnipeds—are mammalian carnivores adapted for life in water. However, they have not entirely forsaken land, to which they return both to give birth and to mate.

IT'S A FACT
The southern elephant seal grows up to 20 feet (6 m) long and 3.7 tons (tonnes) in weight. In previous centuries, before hunting for their oil reduced populations, some may have reached 30 feet (9 m) and 5 tons (tonnes).

Elephant seal

Fur seal

Leopard seal

some showing primitive characteristics, others showing that seals have been around for millions of years. *Enaliarctos*, a primitive sea lion, is one of the earliest known pinnipeds. It lived 25 million years ago.

Pinnipeds feed on fish, squid, and other invertebrates. Many take a variety of food, but there are specialists, such as the crabeater seal of the Antarctic, that feed on krill. Elephant seals have a fondness for squid. The only seal to feed regularly on warm-blooded prey is the leopard seal, up to 11 feet (3.4 m) long, that includes penguins and crabeater seals in its diet. Walruses dive to the bottom to eat invertebrates. They swallow soft ones whole and suck shellfish out of their shells.

Although they breathe out before diving, some pinnipeds can dive for an hour. Their heart rate slows right down underwater. The nostrils can be shut. The ear openings are small, but the sense of hearing remains good.

IT'S A FACT
The crabeater is the commonest seal, and may be the most numerous large mammal in the world. It is estimated that there are 40 million in existence. Since whales have been reduced through hunting and eat fewer krill, crabeaters may have increased in number.

Crabeater seal

Walrus (left)
Walrus tusks are used in fighting and display, and sometimes to help the animal haul itself out of the water. They are not used in feeding.

© DIAGRAM

Otters are members of the same family as weasels and badgers, but they have specialized in living an amphibious life in and around water. Their feet are webbed to a greater or lesser extent, and the tail is flat on the underside and, in some kinds, above as well.

ALTHOUGH they have a long, smooth, and streamlined shape, otters lack the fat layer found in many aquatic mammals, and rely on their dense fur to repel water and keep an insulating layer of air above the skin. The hairs on the snout are developed into long stiff whiskers, and these vibrissae help the otter find food, and feel its way in water where visibility is low. Similar sensory hairs are important to other aquatic mammals such as seals.

The twelve species of otter live in the rivers, lakes, and streams of all the continents except Antarctica and Australia, and some species swim in seawater close to coasts too. Most are active animals and strong swimmers. They stay close to water, although they are quite capable of crossing land at speed. They feed on a range of fish, crayfish, and frogs, but most kinds take whatever food is easiest to catch. Most catch food with their mouths, chopping it if necessary with sharp cheek teeth, but the African clawless otter and the Asian short-clawed otter use their front feet to grab food. They also search crevices with their "hands," which, especially in the clawless otter, are good at grasping and manipulating prey.

The Asian short-clawed otter is the smallest, up to about 3 feet (90 cm) long including tail, and no heavier than a domestic cat. The longest is the South American giant otter, up to 6 feet (1.8 m) long overall and 66 pounds (30 kg) in weight. The sea otter is another big creature, with a

Adapted for swimming
Otters swim by moving their tails and hind feet. They rarely go far from water, and most of their food is fish, frogs, crayfish, and other small water animals.

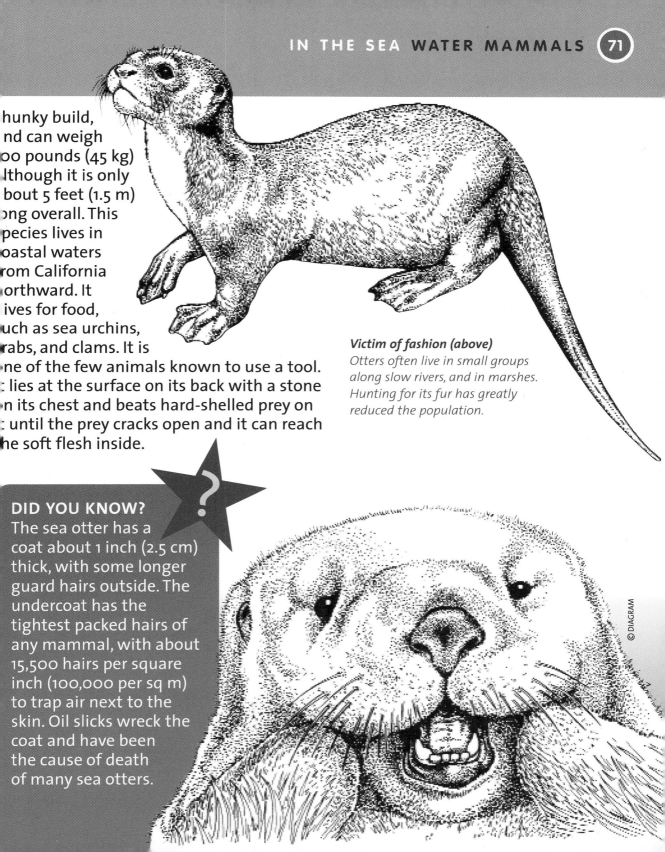

hunky build,
nd can weigh
oo pounds (45 kg)
lthough it is only
bout 5 feet (1.5 m)
ong overall. This
pecies lives in
oastal waters
rom California
orthward. It
ives for food,
uch as sea urchins,
rabs, and clams. It is
ne of the few animals known to use a tool.
: lies at the surface on its back with a stone
n its chest and beats hard-shelled prey on
: until the prey cracks open and it can reach
he soft flesh inside.

Victim of fashion (above)
*Otters often live in small groups
along slow rivers, and in marshes.
Hunting for its fur has greatly
reduced the population.*

DID YOU KNOW?

The sea otter has a
coat about 1 inch (2.5 cm)
thick, with some longer
guard hairs outside. The
undercoat has the
tightest packed hairs of
any mammal, with about
15,500 hairs per square
inch (100,000 per sq m)
to trap air next to the
skin. Oil slicks wreck the
coat and have been
the cause of death
of many sea otters.

© DIAGRAM

In addition to the entire groups of mammals, such as whales or seals, that have become aquatic, many other groups contain mammals that have adapted to make use of water.

Designing the environment
Because of its habit of felling small trees and building dams, a colony of beavers can alter the landscape.

THE MOST PRIMITIVE mammals of all—the egg-laying monotremes—are a tiny group with two kinds of spiny anteater, both very much land animals, and the duckbilled platypus, which is highly adapted to water. The platypus has well-developed webbing on its feet. The front ones do most of the work of paddling. The tail is flattened horizontally. Although young platypuses have a few teeth, they disappear before adulthood, leaving horny plates to crush the food. The snout is covered with sensitive skin, which allows the animal to search out crayfish, shrimps, small fish, worms, and insect larvae. The snout is also equipped with electric organs that detect prey. The fur is very dense, and traps air to act as insulation as the platypus forages in streams. Although this animal is "primitive,"

Survivor
Highly adapted for swimming and finding food in water, the platypus survives from an ancient group of egg-laying mammals.

IT'S A FACT
The duckbilled platypus grows up to 2 feet (60 cm) long overall, and up to 4.5 pounds (2 kg) in weight. It digs a narrow burrow up to 60 feet (18 m) long and, by squeezing into this, forces water from its fur. The male has a large spur on each ankle connected to a venom gland. The female carries wet leaves tucked under the tail to make a nest in the burrow. She lays two eggs that stick together, and feeds the babies on milk for up to four months.

Yapok (above)
This aquatic marsupial, which builds its den in the banks of streams, comes out at night to hunt, but also spends some time on land.

Pyrenean desman (below)
This small insectivore swims well in fast streams with its combination of dense fur and webbed feet.

it is obviously well adapted for its way of life. Platypuses have had a long time to evolve, as fossils go back millions of years. A fossil believed to be part of a platypus has been found in 60-million-year-old rocks in South America. Now monotremes occur only in Australasia.

The pouched mammals, the marsupials, have only one living species that is aquatic, the yapok or water opossum. It lives in freshwater streams and lakes in tropical Central and South America, where it searches for small prey. The hind feet are well webbed, and paddle the animal along. The dense water-repellent fur helps to keep the head up to breathe. The whiskers on the snout are long. The tail is prehensile, long and narrow, an unusual shape for a swimmer, but yapoks spend some time on land. The pouch of the female yapok faces backward, and can be closed with a strong muscle, so the young, up to five of them, are sealed in while mother swims.

Among the placental mammals, it is mainly land-living groups such as rodents and insectivores that have some aquatic species. Semi-aquatic insectivores include: the European water shrew, with little more than a fringe of hairs on its feet to help it swim; the desmans of Russia and the Pyrenees, with webbed feet and dense fur; and the otter shrews, comparatively large animals that look like little otters but propel themselves through water with strong tails. Aquatic rodents range from the beaver, with webbed feet, flattened tail and dense fur, down to water voles with few aquatic adaptations other than a hairy fringe to the foot.

Water vole (above)
This species is found in and around water in Western Europe.

Otter shrew (above)
Otter shrews live in African streams.

© DIAGRAM

Many birds discovered as fossils are waterbirds. This is not surprising, as some types of watery environment are more likely to allow fossilization of a dead body, especially a small one, than most land environments are.

ON LAND, a carcass is usually destroyed, before it has a chance to fossilize, by predators, carrion feeders, various kinds of weather, and decay. However, a quiet pool, lake, or sea may allow a body to sink into mud where the lack of oxygen and predators slows decay, and allows the process of fossilization. This is what happened to the "first bird," *Archaeopteryx*. Although not itself a waterbird, it died and fell into a muddy lagoon that preserved details of its skeleton and feathers 150 million years ago. It still had teeth and a long bony tail, and was probably a clumsy flyer.

Later birds lost the teeth, which changed to a horny beak over the jaws, and also lost the bony tail. Together with other changes, these losses helped to lighten its body, adapting it better to flying. For example, the breastbone is enlarged for the attachment of big flight muscles. By 85 million years ago, many different kinds of bird were undoubtedly in existence, but some of the best known are sea birds. *Hesperornis* was a large bird, sometimes 6 feet (2 m) long, that swam by using its large hind feet. Rather like a loon or grebe in shape, it was entirely dependent on water, having lost the ability to fly. It had a poorly developed breastbone and was virtually wingless. It still had teeth in its jaws. *Ichthyornis* lived at the same time. It was much smaller and was a good flyer.

The "first bird"
Both the skeleton and feathers of Archaeopteryx were preserved by water and mud.

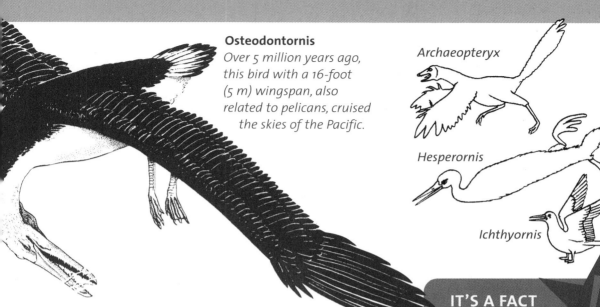

Osteodontornis
Over 5 million years ago, this bird with a 16-foot (5 m) wingspan, also related to pelicans, cruised the skies of the Pacific.

Archaeopteryx

Hesperornis

Ichthyornis

may have been similar in habits, as well as
shape, to a present-day gull or tern, though they are not
closely related.

Before the end of the dinosaur age 65 million years
ago, some familiar types of bird were in existence, such
as loons, early waders, rails, and cormorants. By 50
million years ago stilts, early flamingo relatives, cranes,
gulls, and herons were leaving their bones. Ducks were
living 40 million years ago, and penguins by 20 million
years ago. By 5 million years ago, most of the sea birds
were types we might
recognize today, although
the actual species may
have been different.

Plotopterid
*A relative of pelicans, it
used its wings
to hunt under
water.*

IT'S A FACT
The feet of
Hesperornis were
large. Of the three
forward-facing toes,
the inner one was
comparatively short,
the outer one very
long, unlike the more
symmetrical feet of
most contemporary
aquatic birds. The feet
were good for
swimming, but it is
doubtful whether or
not the bird managed
to stand erect.

© DIAGRAM

Hesperornis

Numerous birds live at the edge of lakes and seas, or in the shallows of rivers. These are places where small invertebrates, small fish, and some kinds of plant life are abundant. This is a huge food resource, used by hundreds of species of bird including groups related to the gulls that are designated "waders" or "shorebirds," herons, flamingos, storks, and ibises.

THE FEET of wading birds are adapted to the area of the water they inhabit, though the need to spread their weight on soft ground is a common feature. Plovers hunt at the very edge of the water, so they have relatively short toes, while herons and storks, which wade further into the water, have long toes. Flamingos have webbed feet. Jacanas, which walk across the surface of lily pads and other floating vegetation looking for food, have the longest toes of all. Leg length also varies depending on feeding area: some birds feed at the edge of the tide, and only need short limbs, whereas others, such as stilts, stand in deeper water and have legs to match. Herons, storks, and flamingos can go even deeper if necessary.

Just as wading birds partition the feeding areas by the length of their legs, they also divide up the available food by having bills of different lengths that probe into the mud or sand to different depths. A further division is made by having beaks with shapes designed for

The right bill for the job
Contrasting shapes enable birds to capture different types of food, and avoid competition while feeding.

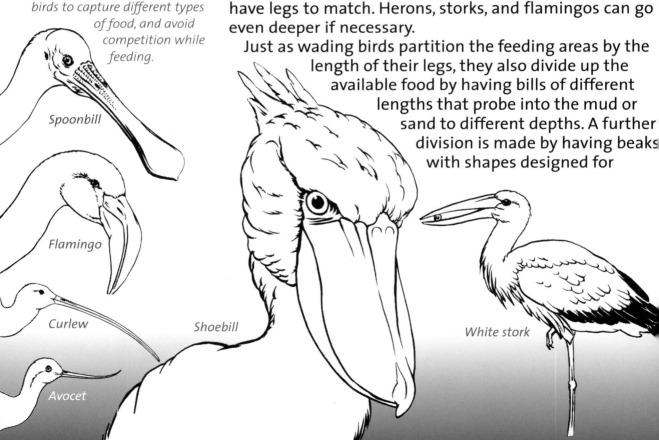

Spoonbill

Flamingo

Curlew

Avocet

Shoebill

White stork

feeding on only certain types of food. Birds such as the African open-billed stork are extreme specialists, feeding on one type of snail, cutting out the muscle with the tip of the bill. Flamingos have bills that form horny filters inside. They take in water or mud, and expel it via the filters which extract the algae or tiny crustaceans on which they feed.

Taking refreshment
Flamingos put their beaks upside down in the water, and their tongues pump water through their filtering mechanism.

IT'S A FACT ●
The wrybill, a New Zealand wader of the plover family, has a beak that points off-center at about 12 degrees to the right. This may be an adaptation to a particular way of feeding—but we don't know what it is.

poonbills sweep the surface of the water for small rey, using their flattened bills. Their relatives, he ibises, probe mud and plants for small nimals. The shoebill stork as a huge flattened bill o catch frogs and fish, ncluding lungfish hat it digs from he mud.

Trotting on lilies
The jacana's long toes disperse its body weight so that it can walk on floating vegetation.

© DIAGRAM

Kingfisher

A number of birds use water as a food source without ever becoming swimmers or waders.

Osprey

THE OSPREY is a hawk that has become expert at snatching large fish from surface waters on the wing, often just dipping its sharp-scaled feet and claws into the water to seize prey. Several species of owl practice a similar method of feeding at night, catching fish in their talons.

Other hunters use their bills to catch prey from water. The kingfisher perches on a branch, or hovers above a river, then plunges to seize a small fish in its beak. Out at sea, albatrosses glide above the waves for months on end, patrolling the ocean, only sometimes dipping their beaks to catch a fish or squid. Occasionally they plunge to catch fish. Gannets are the expert at plunging for fish, flying high to spot a meal, then darting down, folding their wings as they hit the water.

Skimmers, which hunt over still water, have extraordinary beaks in which the bottom jaw is much longer than the top. They fly with the sharp tip of the lower beak skimming the surface of the water. Touching a small fish, they drop the jaw and snap up a victim. All these are efficient hunters, but are scarcely swimmers.

The duck family contains birds that are mostly at home floating on the water, with waterproof plumage and large webbed feet with which to paddle. Even here, there are a variety of feeding methods.

Skimmer

Mallards upend and pull vegetation and small animals from the water. Some species of swan, too, are expert at stretching their necks down to water vegetation. Shoveler ducks have broad flat bills and constantly dip them at the surface to catch small animals and plants. Tufted ducks make short dives below the surface for food. Pelicans are good swimmers—like most of their relatives they have all four toes in a foot web. Most species swim at the surface and use the pouch below the beak as a fishing net to scoop up prey. Some kinds cooperate to drive fish into a tight group that can be caught more easily. The American brown pelican, though, dives like a gannet to catch food.

The darters swim very low in the water, with just the top of the back and the rather reptilian head showing, hence their second name of snakebirds. A darter slowly stalks prey in still, open water, then suddenly shoots its beak out to stab a fish. This is shaken off the beak and then swallowed head first.

IT'S A FACT
A pelican can hold more in its beak than in its belly. It has a very large throat pouch, but rarely holds food in it for long before swallowing. When it catches fish, the pouch fills with water that may weigh more than the pelican. This needs to be expelled before swallowing food or attempting to fly.

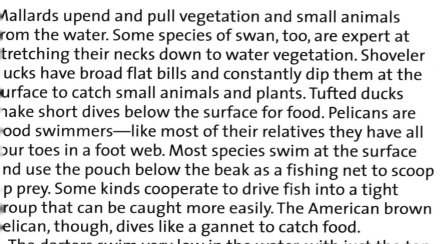

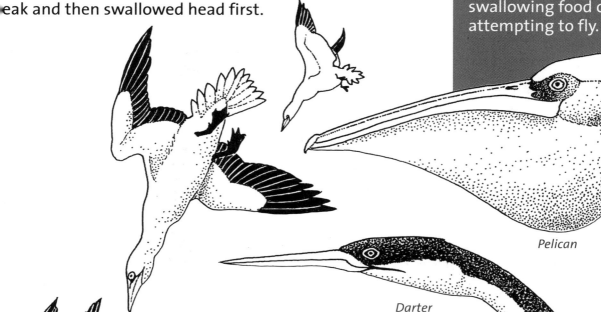

Pelican

Gannets

Darter

Shoveler

© DIAGRAM

Of all birds, the 16 species of penguins are best adapted to diving and swimming under water. They have a torpedo-shaped body. The wings are used under water to "fly" as other birds use their wings in air but, in this denser medium, the wings need to be shorter and stiffer.

PENGUINS cannot fly, but are fantastic swimmers. They are very well adapted to a life in water. The plumage is short, oily, very dense, and waterproof. A layer of fat under the skin helps insulation. Several heat-exchange arrangements in the blood system also keep heat in. For example, in the nasal passages, four-fifths of the heat in the exhaled air is kept in the body rather than lost to the outside air.

All this is necessary as penguins are birds of cold, southern waters. Some species live in and around the Antarctic. Even those that live on the coasts of Africa, South America, and on the equator at the Galapagos Islands, are in places where cold currents sweep the coastlines, bringing with them a copious supply of plankton and fish to eat.

A unique design
Penguins stand upright because their feet are set so far back on their torsos. Their webbed feet are very effective for steering in water.

IT'S A FACT
Penguins and many auks have dark backs and white fronts, colors that make them inconspicuous in water. The colors that show which species they belong to are often on the head and neck, the parts that are above water, and easy to see when the birds are at the surface.

King penguin

Chinstrap

Rockhopper

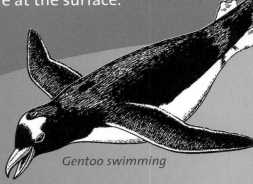
Gentoo swimming

The bones of penguins are more solid than those of most birds. Their bodies are almost as dense as seawater, which makes diving considerably easier. Most penguins dive for only a minute or two, but the largest species, the emperor penguin, has been timed diving for 18 minutes, and to a depth of 860 feet (260 m).

Apart from penguins, divers among the birds include the loons (divers), and the grebes. Both groups are foot-propelled, with large feet set right at the back of the body. They can hardly move on land, and stay on water when they are not nesting. On the other hand, their wings are normal bird wings that allow them to fly well. They are efficient hunters of fish and other small water animals.

In the Northern Hemisphere, the counterparts of the penguins are the auks—puffins, razorbill, and guillemots. These relatives of the gulls have fairly chunky, streamlined bodies, and swim well using their wings for propulsion. Although their wings are short they still work in air, and auks are good flyers, although their wingbeats are very rapid to keep them in the air. The exception was the flightless great auk, a bird that weighed up to 18 pounds (8 kg). Hunters killed the last of this species in 1844.

Hunted to extinction
Able to swim well, but flightless, the great auk was doomed when human hunters raided its nesting grounds.

Atlantic puffin (below)
This bird catches small fish, such as sand eels, and may carry several across its beak.

©DIAGRAM

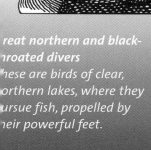

Great northern and black-throated divers
These are birds of clear, northern lakes, where they pursue fish, propelled by their powerful feet.

The seashore is one of the most challenging environments for life because conditions are always changing. Between high tide and low tide, animals and algae are covered by the sea for part of the day, but then may be exposed, drying in the sun and air, or trapped in pools which warm up, evaporate, and become increasingly salty, until the tide comes in again. They are also buffeted by the waves.

MANY OF THE ANIMALS on a rocky shore have hard shells for protection, for example, periwinkles, whelks, and top shells. They often hide in pools or crevices when the tide goes out. Limpets' muscles clamp them to the rock when the tide goes out. When it comes in again they leave their resting place and roam the rock surfaces grazing algae. Barnacles, too, shut down when they are left dry, but open up to feed with kicking legs when the tide is in. Mussels are fixed to rocks by threads that they produce, but only open when the sea covers them. Sea anemones, sponges, sea squirts, and other soft-bodied animals survive in the more sheltered parts of the rocky shore. Although it is a hard environment, a rocky shore provides many kinds of living space, and a surprising number of species live here. Often a series of

Meiofauna (right)
In between mud or sand particles on the seashore live tiny, elongated animals which can usually grow to 0.004–0.08 inches (0.1–2.0 mm) in overall length.

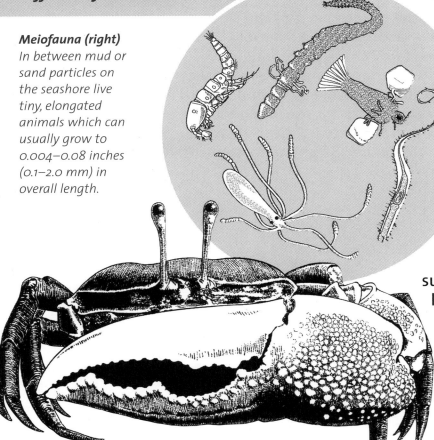

Fiddler crabs (left)
These creatures live in burrows in the intertidal zone. When the tide is out, they come out to feed. Males have one enlarged claw used primarily in courtship rituals.

ones can be seen on a rocky shore, with different animals nd seaweeds adapted to their differing conditions.

Sandy and muddy shores provide different challenges. The ea scours these each day, and seaweeds and surface-living nimals are rare. Underground, worms, crabs, and shellfish, uch as sand gapers and razor clams, populate the sand. They ften stay in the sand, only pushing breathing tubes or eeding tentacles up to the surface. Not many kinds of nimals like these conditions, but those that can survive may ften be present in large numbers.

Many of the seashore animals produce eggs or larvae that re released into the sea and become part of the floating lankton, untold numbers perishing before a few settle on nother rocky shore and mature. Some animals, such as onger eels and edible crabs, may be found in the lower parts f the tidal region as small adults, but move further offshore s they mature.

IT'S A FACT
The greatest tidal range can be found in the Bay of Fundy, Nova Scotia, where the difference between high and low tide can be 50 feet (15 m). Other parts of the world may only have a range of 3 feet (1 m) between high and low tides.

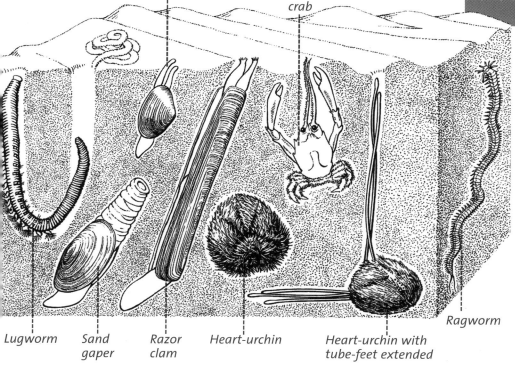

Tellin   Masked crab

Dwellers on the seashore
On a sandy shore, the animals live down damp burrows when the tide is out. Many are filter feeders, coming to the sand surface to breathe and feed, when the ocean tide comes in.

Lugworm   Sand gaper   Razor clam   Heart-urchin   Heart-urchin with tube-feet extended   Ragworm

© DIAGRAM

Although some types of coral do grow in cool seas, typical coral reefs are found in warm tropical seas with water between 65°F (18°C) and 85°F (30°C). They grow best in clear water at about 74–77°F (23–25°C) and are not found where rivers discharge silt into the sea.

A CORAL REEF is made of the skeletons of millions of small coral polyps. These small animals lay down a little calcium carbonate each day, building up a skeleton below and around them. The shape of the skeleton varies between species, some colonies being domes, others tree or fanlike. Some corals die, others grow on top. The net result is a build-up of a big reef of calcium carbonate with a thin skin of living tissue, the coral polyps, on the outside. The coral polyps live in a partnership with tiny single-celled algae. Algae within the polyps make food from sunlight and carbon dioxide, some of which comes from the host polyp. The polyps make use of some of the simple sugars and oxygen that the algae produce. Since these corals need the light, they can grow no deeper than about 165 feet (50 m), so are found fairly close to shore.

In fact there are, as Charles Darwin set out in the 1840s, several recognizable types of reef, but they all result from the predictable way that coral grows. A fringing reef grows close to land, but the coral polyps use their tentacles to catch tiny plankton, and this is most abundant on the seaward side. The reef tends to grow fast on this side, but may die off on the

New volcanic island

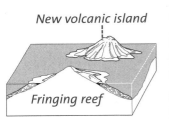

Fringing reef

Barrier reef

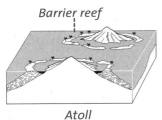

Atoll

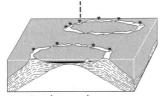

Sunken volcano

Coral reef formations
Coral grows where the sea is shallow. The Great Barrier Reef, situated off the coast of northern Australia, comprises millions of tiny coral polyps.

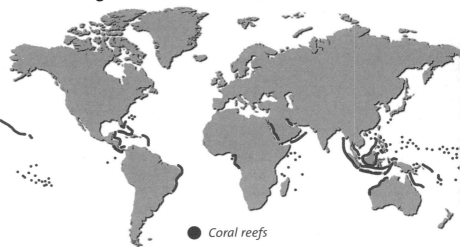

● *Coral reefs*

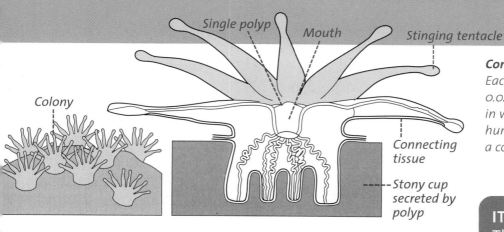

Single polyp | Mouth | Stinging tentacle

Colony

Connecting tissue

Stony cup secreted by polyp

Coral polyps
Each coral polyp is only 0.04–0.12 inches (1–3 mm) in width, but there may be hundreds or thousands in a colony.

landward side. Gradually the reef moves to become a barrier reef at some distance from land. This progression can be seen on many volcanic islands in the Pacific. In some cases the volcanic island slowly sinks below the waves, but the coral reef keeps growing up toward the surface. This results in an atoll, a ring of coral with no land left in the center, although there may be a build-up of coral debris and sand within that makes the lagoon shallow.

The coral reef built originally by the polyps becomes one of the most complex habitats on Earth, with a multitude of animals making use of the many different types of space and ways of feeding that are on offer. The range of species found there compares to the most complex habitat on land—the tropical rainforest.

IT'S A FACT
The corals of each species in an area release their eggs and sperm on the same day—a little after the full moon. This ensures the maximum chance of fertilization for these animals, unable to move and search for a mate. Fertilized eggs begin to develop, and soon the coral larvae settle on the reef to fight for space.

Types of coral
"Brain" corals, "tables," and branching forms are among the many shapes of coral colonies.

© DIAGRAM

FISHES, AS WELL AS MAMMALS, feed on coral. Butterfly fish, for example, pick off coral polyps and other small creatures from the reef using their long snouts and brushlike teeth. Parrot fish have beaklike front teeth, and a grinding apparatus of teeth in their throats. Some fish are entirely plant-eating, but others cut off small chunks of coral, skeleton and all, and grind them to extract nourishment.

Many wrasses pick off small animals from coral or rocks with their front teeth and grind crabs and shellfish in their throats. Other fish, such as goatfish, grub on the bottom with their sensory barbels (whiskers) and suck up small fish that they find. A whole host of fish from small gobies to huge groupers are hunters, as are crabs, mantis shrimps, starfish, and some mollusks. When night time comes, a whole new set of hunters comes out to roam the reef, including moray eels and some sharks—both fishes with good scenting ability to find prey that has hidden in crevices for the night.

Plant eaters on the reef include many kinds of fish,

Parrot fish
This species has distinctive beaklike jaws, which give it its unusual name.

Helping each other
Many coral shrimps act as cleaners for fish with parasites or wounds.

IT'S A FACT

One of the most specialized jobs on the reef is that of cleaner. Cleaner wrasses live in one place and advertise their presence. Other fishes, including many that would consume a fish the size of a wrasse, come to the cleaning station and wait patiently with mouth and gills spread for the cleaner fish to pick off parasites from their skin—sometimes even from inside the mouth and gills. Some shrimp species also function as cleaners, acquiring the same immunity from attack by predators. Cleaners provide a vital service.

IT'S A FACT

The crown of thorns starfish turns its stomach inside out over the coral polyps to digest them. Normally these starfish exist in numbers which do the reef no long-term damage overall, but at least twice in the 20th century "plagues" of starfish have reduced large areas of reef to bleached white skeletons.

such as surgeonfish and damselfish, and, on Atlantic reefs, sea urchins. A number of fish also wait for the plankton that is carried to the reef, as do basket stars, spreading their feathery arms to trap prey, and the corals themselves.

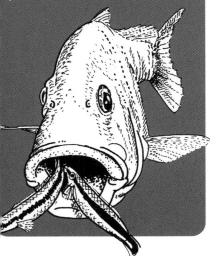

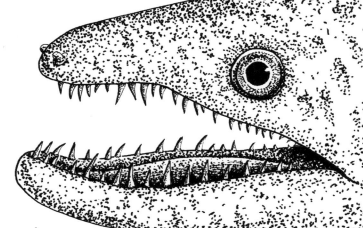

Moray eel
These hide in crevices, and come out at night to hunt.

Plankton, floating sea life at the mercy of the elements, exist in the top layers of the sea. Light penetrates and allows cyanobacteria and algae to photosynthesize. Only the top 600 feet (180 m), even in the clearest seas, is light enough for "plants." However, not all areas of the sea are equally productive.

AREAS WHERE CURRENTS WELL UP, carrying nutrients from the deep, grow more plankton than other parts of the ocean do. Most tropical waters have fewer nutrients than many temperate seas, which have the highest densities of plankton, particularly in spring and early summer. There can be over 400 million tiny plants in a cubic yard (meter) of water. Virtually all the "plants" in the sea are in the plankton, and all other life in the sea depends, directly or indirectly, on them. The seaweeds that grow on the coasts are comparatively unimportant.

Plankton animals eat plankton "plants." Some small crustaceans, such as copepods, live permanently in the plankton. Other plankton animals are larvae of crabs, fish, worms, starfish, or jellyfish that spend their adult lives elsewhere. Some eat "plant" plankton directly, others feed on smaller animals in the plankton. Plankton also provide food for fishes such as herring, anchovy, and mackerel. Some plankton feeders spend the day deeper, and rise to the top layers to feed at night, when they are probably safer from larger predators. Basking sharks and some of the great whales depend on plankton, too.

The middle zone of the sea contains shoals of fish, such as tuna and barracuda,

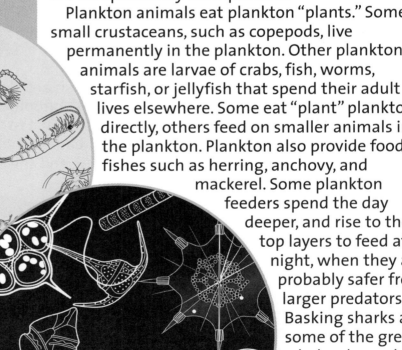

Zooplankton (above)
These tiny, floating animals include copepods, and barnacle and worm larvae.

Phytoplankton (right)
Diatoms are single-celled "plants" with silica shells.

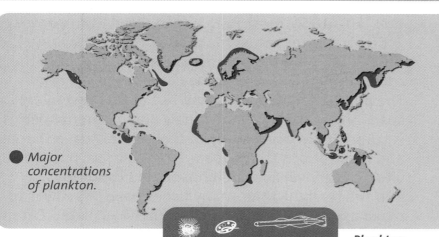

● *Major concentrations of plankton.*

Plankton
Organisms of different groups can be found at the sea's surface.

streamlined fast swimmers that are active predators, as well as sharks. Some squid are fast swimmers and ferocious predators, and also live in the middle zone.

Some animals defend themselves against these predators by having spines or stings. Many fish gain protection by living in a shoal that moves and makes sudden changes of direction together, making it hard for a predator to single out a victim.

Areas of productivity in the sea change as the seasons progress. Herring shoals migrate back and forth, following the areas where plankton is most abundant. Larger carnivores, such as tuna, cross the width of the Atlantic or Pacific Oceans as they follow their prey.

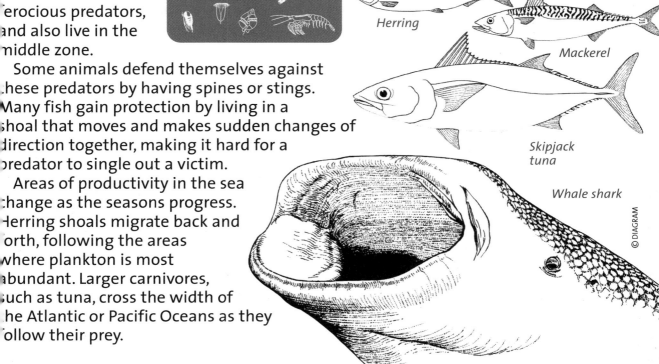

Herring

Mackerel

Skipjack tuna

Whale shark

© DIAGRAM

Below the sunlight zone of the sea, there is a twilight zone where very faint light may penetrate no more than 3,000 feet (1,000 m) down. Below there is inky darkness, where the water is just above freezing point and the pressure is enormous.

IN THE ABYSS, most food has to come from above. Creatures here must make use of the slow rain of dead animals and plants, fragments, and feces that come from above, or else they must eat each other. The population density is low, but in this vast living space the number of individuals and different species is surprisingly large. Many of the animals have shapes and adaptations that appear strange to us, but are vital for survival in such inhospitable conditions.

In the twilight zone, many fishes have large eyes to make use of the tiny amounts of light available. Often the eyes are directed up, to see food coming down or spot prey against the faint light from the surface. Squid in this zone also have large eyes. One type, *Histioteuthis*, has one huge eye, and one smaller. It is believed to hang in the water with its large eye looking upward.

In the black depths, eyes have nothing to see most of the time, and fishes and other animals tend to have small eyes. Many of the animals in this region, however, make their own light from specialized organs. Lights may be used as signals to locate others of their kind, or

Viperfish (left)
The teeth of this fish can seize any prey it happens to encounter.

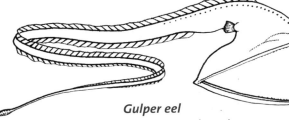

Gulper eel
A huge mouth and an expandable stomach allow it to capture large prey.

sometimes, perhaps, to confuse predators. Some, such as anglerfishes, use light as a "lure" on the fishing-rod tentacles in front of their heads.

In the deep an animal rarely encounters a potential meal. It has to seize any opportunity that arises. Many deepwater fishes have huge mouths, ferocious teeth, and stomachs that stretch to hold prey as big as or bigger than themselves. Most of these fish, in spite of their strange and ferocious appearance, are only 1 foot (30 cm) long or less. They also have strangely frail bodies. Always surrounded by water, hardly ever coming into contact with anything solid, they do not need a rugged build. They spend a lot of time more or less immobile, waiting for a meal. Some have well-developed touch sensors—either their lateral line or tentacles—to help detect their prey.

STRANGE BUT TRUE

Anglerfish have solved the problem of finding a mate at the right time. A male anglerfish has no role in life, once hatched, other than to swim to find a female. He then bites into her body and becomes fused to her as a parasite. The male is tiny compared to the female. He not only receives nourishment from her, but also provides sperm at egg-laying time.

Diaphus
A lantern fish with luminous organs.

Anglerfish
A lure above its head entices prey to its traplike jaws.

© DIAGRAM

At the bottom of the ocean, much of the floor is flat and featureless. Even here, animals survive. The mud contains single-celled animals, small worms and small, bivalve mollusks. On the surface of the mud there are sea cucumbers, brittle stars, and sea urchins. Sponges also live here. All these depend on particles that have drifted down from above.

EVEN IN THE DEEPEST PARTS of the ocean, there is life. Fishes, such as rat-tails, scavenge for food. Most fish species of the ocean floor have to be more robust than those above, due to the inhospitable conditions of the abyss. Some, however, are more delicate, such as the tripod fish that stands on three stilts made from long fin rays, waiting for food to pass by.

It is not on the flat ocean floor, though, that the most surprising creatures are found, but at the submarine mountain chains that form mid-ocean ridges. Here the sea floor is studded with areas where water seeps into the earth. It is heated to enormous temperatures and bubbles up again, carrying volcanic material. Clouds of water full of sulfurous chemicals pour from small vents. Towers build up around them as chemicals crystallize. Although the temperature

A different world
Energy from volcanic vents powers an abundance of life different from forms seen at the surface.

Small vent animals
Many animals, including specialized shrimps and crabs, can be found close to hot vents.

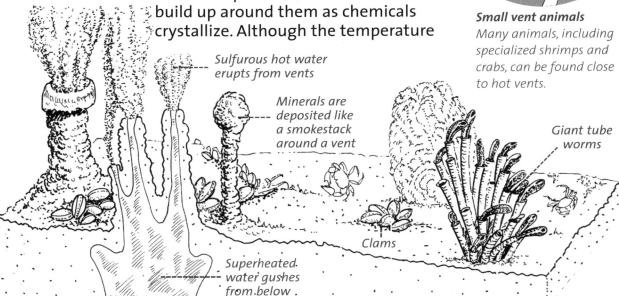

Sulfurous hot water erupts from vents

Minerals are deposited like a smokestack around a vent

Giant tube worms

Clams

Superheated water gushes from below

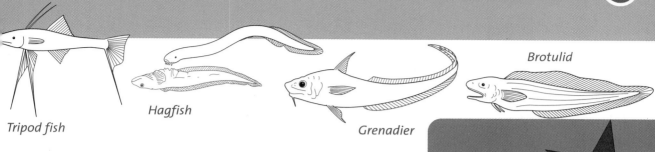

Tripod fish

Hagfish

Grenadier

Brotulid

of the water can be up to 750°F (400°C), the pressure is so great that it does not turn to steam. These are not conditions in which life would thrive with any degree of success.

However, around the hydrothermal vents a rich collection of creatures has been discovered. Instead of finding the hydrogen sulfide gushing from the vents poisonous, as most living things would, some of the life here actually uses it as a source of energy. Huge tubeworms, up to 6 feet (2 m) long, live by hydrothermal vents in the Pacific. However, they have no mouth or gut. More than half their bodyweight consists of bacteria that can use hydrogen sulfide to manufacture the organic matter that life requires. Clams and mussels living nearby are also full of these bacteria, although the mussels still have mouths and can feed in the normal way. In the Atlantic, vents provide a rich source of sulfide for bacteria, and shrimps feed on bacteria at the start of the ocean food chain.

Since the ocean floor hydrothermal vents were discovered in 1979, hundreds of new species have been found around them. They are one of the world's richest ecosystems. Some scientists believe they may give us insights into how life functioned when it first evolved on Earth.

STRANGE BUT TRUE
By hydrothermal vents near the Galapagos Islands lives a white tubeworm with the ability to survive higher temperatures than any other animal. It normally lives at 150°F (65°C), yet can also survive short spells at 175°F (80°C).

Sea cucumber
An animal related to sea urchins, it moves across the seabed collecting food particles.

© DIAGRAM

Antarctica is a large continent surrounded by a very cold sea. At the northern pole there is sea, but parts of the northern continents project into the Arctic Circle.

THERE ARE AREAS OF PERMANENT SEA ICE at both the Antarctic and Arctic, surrounded by areas where during the brief summer the ice melts, only to freeze again as winter sets in. Even in summer, the water is scarcely above freezing point. In spite of this, there is a surprising amount of life. Planktonic plants, diatoms, live in the sea ice and can survive the winter. Other microscopic creatures and small crustaceans live there, too. When spring comes and the amount of light increases, there is a bloom of plant plankton, followed by an increase in animal plankton, then by an influx of animals migrating in to feed.

The Weddell seal lives under the Antarctic sea ice, relying on its round shape, padded out by a thick layer of blubber, to stay warm. It needs to breathe air, so it cannot always remain submerged. It has a breathing hole through the ice, and keeps this from freezing over by gnawing the edge with its teeth. Unfortunately, this can lead to dental problems that stop the seal living to a ripe old age.

Many animals of the polar seas use chemicals as "antifreeze" in their bodies. In winter, limpets on Antarctic shores move to greater depths out of the way of ice, and secrete antifreeze

Weddell seal
The most southerly-dwelling mammal, it grows to 10 feet (3 m) long, and can reach 1,000 pounds (450 kg) in weight.

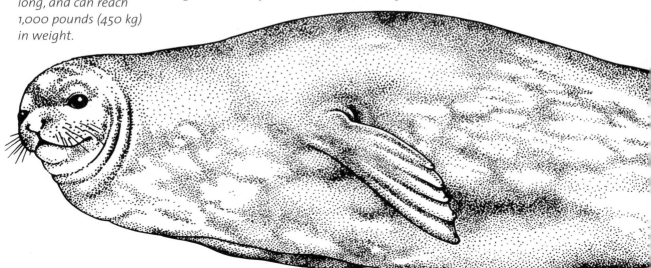

Icefish
Only a small number of species of fish can live in the freezing waters of the Antarctic.

slime around their bodies. Antifreeze is found in some Arctic fishes, and is common in Antarctic fishes. Molecules of the chemical attach to ice crystals that are forming, and stop them developing further. The ice fish of the Antarctic have no hemoglobin (red pigment) in their blood, and are very pale creatures. In the cold, oxygen-filled waters they can manage without red blood, but are sluggish animals with bodies that work slowly.

The seabed below the ice is home to many animals. In the cold water they may grow slowly, but some eventually become large, such as yard-long (1 m) ribbon worms. Starfish, sea urchins, crabs and smaller crustaceans, many bivalve mollusks, and sea anemones are among those creatures living in seas that are frozen at the surface.

IT'S A FACT
Some adult krill spend winter under the ice, living on fat accumulated in summer, with their bodies working much more slowly than in the summer. Crustaceans usually molt and develop new skins as they grow larger. Krill, in winter, reverse this process. They molt and become smaller. In spring, when food becomes available, they grow yet again.

In streams and rivers the water is always on the move, but a slow-flowing, lowland river is very different from a stream at its source in the hills. Near the source the stream is often fast-flowing, sometimes a torrent carrying stones and boulders along.

IN FAST-FLOWING STREAMS, it is difficult for anything to acquire a foothold. Plants are just an algal slime on the rocks. Strong-swimming fish, such as trout, may be able to remain stationary, and eat insects carried down by the stream. In various parts of the world, fishes in hill streams have adapted to the conditions by becoming flattened, living on the bottom or under stones, or making use of suckers to hold on. Sometimes the mouth forms a sucker, as in loaches. In other cases, such as the Bornean sucker fish, the paired fins are enlarged and flattened to form an adhesive disc. Southeast Asian torrent frog tadpoles have suckers below their mouths.

A few insects can hold on in fast streams. Stonefly nymphs have long legs with strong claws, and flat bodies. Some caddisfly larvae spin silk to help them stay in one place. Some species even spin nets to catch food swept down by the current. Blackfly larvae cling on using hooks at the back of their bodies.

A few birds are adapted for foraging in fast streams. As the dipper walks underwater, head down and wings partly up, the current it is walking against helps it to keep its grip.

Changing inhabitants
As a stream makes its way to the sea, species adapted to fast-flowing water, such as dipper and trout, give way to species adapted to slow-flowing water.

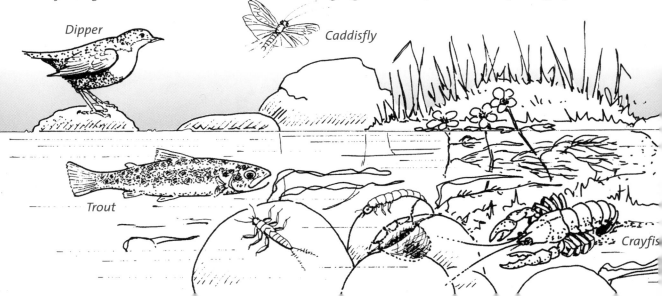

Dipper

Caddisfly

Trout

Crayfis

Adapted for survival
Torrent ducks can swim against the flow of the rapids of South American rivers when looking for food underwater.

As the stream goes further down its course, it slows and more kinds of animal can survive. Various snails and mussels, plus mayfly nymphs, and dragonfly and beetle larvae can live here. Fish here do not need to be strong swimmers, and minnows and other streamlined fishes are to be found. Lower down still, the river slows and may meander across lowlands. Often many plants will be able to grow, and slower-swimming, deep-bodied fish such as roach, carp, and green sunfish swim between them, feeding from the river bottom. The warmer, slower water contains less oxygen than the mountain stream, but the plants compensate by releasing some. The insect inhabitants of the slowest rivers are similar to those of lakes and ponds.

DID YOU KNOW?
Freshwater crayfish are relatives of the lobster. They live in slow-flowing streams and rivers in hard-water areas. They need plenty of calcium in the water to form their shells. There are about 500 species worldwide.

Bornean sucker fish
The whole of the underside of the body is turned into a sucker to grip the rocks in torrential rivers.

Stickleback

Roach

Snail

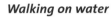

Walking on water
*The pond skater is one of
the insects that can walk
on water.*

*Ponds are small, shallow bodies of
water. They may fill with water in
wet periods, and evaporate to a
low level, or even to nothing, in
hot dry periods. Lakes are larger,
deeper bodies of water. Unlike
ponds, where vegetation may
grow over much of the area, some
lakes are so deep that plants grow
only at the edges.*

PONDS CAN BE DIFFICULT PLACES TO
LIVE, and animals may need special
strategies to survive. Some shrimps, for
example, hatch in temporary pools in desert
areas after rains, and complete their whole
life cycle in just a few weeks, laying eggs that can survive,
dried out, for months, or even years.

The depths of a lake may be very cold, and most of the life is
near the surface. Nevertheless, lakes support a variety of life.
Some lakes are so big and varied that they have many of their
own species, which are found nowhere else. Some of the lakes
in Africa's Great Rift Valley are home to many different species
of cichlid fish that have evolved there.
Lake Tanganyika holds about 130 species,
plus other special fish of other families. The
huge Lake Baikal in Russia has some 900
species of many animal groups
special to it. It even

Freshwater seal
*Only 4 feet (1.2 m) long,
the Baikal seal is the only
seal restricted to fresh
water. It often swims near
the surface upside down,
looking for fish to eat.*

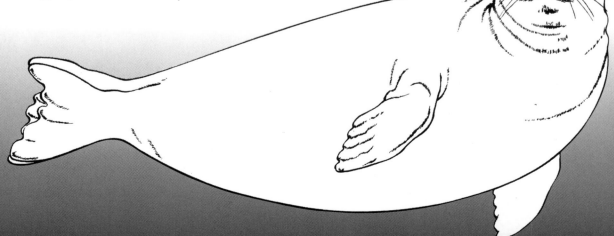

has its own seal, the smallest species known. It is related to an Arctic species, the ringed seal, that probably colonized the lake when the sea was much closer to it.

The still water of ponds provides, for small animals, a habitat that is not available in rougher waters—that is, the water surface as a place to live and hunt. Insects, such as pond skaters, can be seen moving around with ease, catching small prey that have fallen in or approached the surface too closely. The attraction of water molecules for one another is enough, at this scale, to make a platform to walk on, as long as the walker does not attract water itself. A pond skater has wax on its feet that repels water. Although the insect's feet dimple the surface, it is not broken. Some other bugs and beetles use the same trick.

Still fresh waters often have plankton which form the bottom of the food pyramid. Added to this are small animals and food particles falling into the water. In a pond or lake where plankton is constantly growing and being eaten, the bulk of the larger predatory animals can be greater than that of the plankton. This is very different from on land, where predators are almost always fewer, and make up far less bulk, than the living things at the bottom of the food pyramid.

IT'S A FACT
Dragonflies are fearsome predators in ponds and at the edges of lakes. The drably-colored nymph may live in a pond for two years or more before molting and becoming a flying insect. It has long hinged jaws with grasping fangs. Normally folded, this "mask" can be shot out suddenly to catch small fish, tadpoles, and insects.

© DIAGRAM

Lake Nyasa cichlids

A hinged mask shoots forward to grasp prey.

Going home
Most species of salmon are migratory, some making huge journeys to find a breeding ground.

AFTER ANYTHING from one to five years, depending on conditions, the young salmon has made its way to an estuary, where it gets used to salt water before going to sea. Out at sea it grows rapidly, feeding on smaller fish.

After four years at sea, weighing from 30 pounds (14 kg) to even 70 pounds (32 kg), the salmon returns to fresh water to breed. The fish will smell or taste its way back to the exact stream in which it was hatched. The salmon fight their way up, sometimes making huge leaps up waterfalls, to the gravel beds where they spawn. After this effort, many fish are exhausted and some die. Others drift back to sea and feed again before returning to spawn another year. The journeys the salmon make to spawn may be hundreds or even thousands of miles (kilometers).

Salmon are sea fish that migrate into freshwater streams to breed. Their eggs are laid in gravel beds, and hatch in spring as tiny fry that rely on their yolk sacs for nourishment for the first few weeks. Then they start feeding on small invertebrates, and turn into parr, a stage with striped camouflage. These feed and make their way downstream.

IT'S A FACT
The king salmon of the north Pacific swims up rivers to spawn. Those that travel the farthest, up rivers in the Yukon, may spawn as much as 2,250 miles (3,600 km) from the sea.

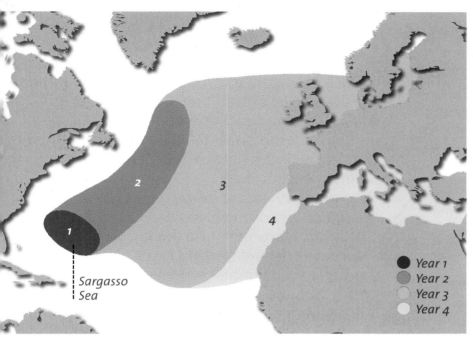

The journey of the eel
Adult eels spawn in the Sargasso Sea, in the middle of the North Atlantic. The map (left) shows the location of the larvae over the next four years on their slow journey to Europe.

Year 1
Year 2
Year 3
Year 4

Sargasso Sea

The European eel is another species which has a migratory pattern linked to breeding. Although familiar as a freshwater species, the eel starts life in salt water, in the Sargasso Sea. The hatchlings grow and drift as larvae in the Gulf Stream toward Europe. At this stage they are not very eel-like, as they are semi-transparent, and flattened from side to side like a leaf.

When it reaches the coasts, an eel changes. Its body becomes rounded and eel-like, and pectoral fins develop. To begin with it is a "glass eel" with a transparent body, then pigment develops and it is an "elver." Both of these forms ascend rivers, and the eels live in fresh water for ten years or more, growing and feeding before it is time to make the journey back across the Atlantic to spawn. Their eyes enlarge, the head shape changes, and they become silvery. The journey takes up to seven months and eels do not feed on the way. How eels find their way back is not known, but the whole life cycle is a remarkable one for a vertebrate. There are so many changes of form, and the journey may cover 3,000 miles (5,000 km) or more each way.

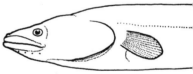

Developing a look
The freshwater eel migrates to the sea to breed. It reaches its breeding grounds as a large-eyed fish.

© DIAGRAM

For animals that are mainly solitary, and spend their adult lives scattered through the oceans, finding a mate and raising offspring could be a problem.

MANY CREATURES solve the problem of finding a mate by congregating at one site during the mating season. Sea birds such as albatrosses, scattered throughout the year, come to a few oceanic islands to breed. Sea lions have favored breeding beaches where they come together for a short season, then disperse for the rest of the year. Sea turtles, too, have favorite breeding grounds.

The green turtle swims through most tropical seas, but breeds in only a few places. In the Atlantic, many green turtles lay their eggs on Ascension Island. Mating takes place offshore, and then the females emerge on the beach, bury their eggs, and return to the water. Each may do this several times during one season. The adult turtles then disperse. Most make for feeding areas off the Brazilian coast over 1,250 miles (2,000 km) away. Next breeding season they travel back again, against the prevailing current. As the current goes about as fast as turtles normally swim, nobody is quite sure how they manage this feat. Perhaps they take a longer, but easier, route. Why do they make these long

Predestination
Green turtles head for the sea instinctively, having just hatched on Ascension Island.

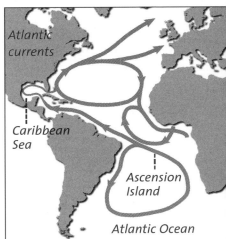

Atlantic currents

Caribbean Sea

Ascension Island

Atlantic Ocean

migrations? Ascension is a good place to breed, but there are other, closer islands that might serve the purpose. The answer may be that this is a very ancient habit indeed, started by turtles many millions of years ago, when South America and Africa had not drifted so far apart. The turtles may have originally had quite a short journey across the Atlantic, but it extends by a few inches (centimeters) each year .

Some whales make long migrations in the course of the year between polar waters and the tropics. Here the reason seems straightforward. They make use of the upsurge in food in polar seas in summer months. Then they travel to warmer waters for the birth of their young, which spend the first weeks of their lives in a place where their comparatively poor insulation is not a problem. The gray whale lives in the seas between Siberia and Alaska from June to October, when the sea begins to ice up. It then swims down the west coast of America and spends winter in warm lagoons off California and Mexico. Here the calves are born in January, and mating takes place. Although the adults find little food at this time of year, a calf feeds on the mother's rich milk and grows fast. By March or April it is able to make the journey north to the summer feeding grounds.

STRANGE BUT TRUE
Some gray whales make a round trip of 12,500 miles (20,000 km) each year.

Gray whale (above)
In the polar seas the gray whale feeds on crustaceans living at the very bottom.

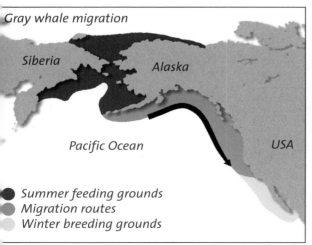

Gray whale migration

Siberia

Alaska

Pacific Ocean

USA

● Summer feeding grounds
● Migration routes
● Winter breeding grounds

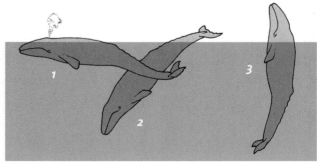

Whales in motion (above)
1 Blowing
2 Diving
3 Spying and hopping

© DIAGRAM

Million years ago	Events
5,000–4,000	**4,550** Formation of the Earth
4,000–3,000	**3,600** Origins of life
3,000–2,000	**2,400** First organisms with a cell nucleus
2,000–1,000	**1,400** First multicellular organisms
1,000–500	**560** First multicellular animals forming communities in the sea
Trilobite	**545** Explosion of life in shallow seas; first shelled animals
	540 First trilobites
500–250	**490** Life spreads to the open ocean
	475 First corals and moss animals
	465 First jawless fish
	455 First land plants
	440 First jawed fish; first placoderm fish
	417 First land animals
Ammonite	**415** First ammonites
	380 Early sharks
	360 First "amphibians"
	350 Rise of ammonites; last placoderm fish; first coelacanths
	325 First reptiles
250–100	**250** Last trilobites; first ichthyosaurs
	240 First modern corals
	210 First mammals; first turtles
Turtle	**200** Rise of plesiosaurs; early salamanders; first frogs
	160 Rise of the teleost ray-finned fishes
100–now	**90** Last ichthyosaurs
	85 Early waterbirds
	80 Heyday of mosasaurs; giant sea lizards
	70 Disappearance of plesiosaurs
	65 Extinction of ammonites and dinosaurs; modern crocodiles evolved
Whales	**55** First whales
	40 First ducks
	25 Early sea lions
	20 Penguins in existence

ossils help scientists determine when different kinds of plants and animals
rst appeared.

Era	Millions of years ago	Period	Main events	
Proterozoic Eon	2,550–543	Proterozoic periods		bacteria, simple animals, and plants exist
Paleozoic	543–490	Cambrian		sea animals without a backbone flourish
	490–443	Ordovician		early fish appear
	443–417	Silurian		land plants and land arthropods appear
	417–354	Devonian		insects and amphibians appear
	354–290	Carboniferous		reptiles and flying insects live in forests
	290–248	Permian		reptiles dominate
Mesozoic	248–206	Triassic		dinosaurs dominate, mammals appear
	206–144	Jurassic		birds appear and pterosaurs flourish
	144–65	Cretaceous		flowering plants appear
Cenozoic	65–1.8	Tertiary		dinosaurs die out, mammals spread
	1.8–present	Quaternary		humans dominate

abyss The bottom of the ocean; adjective **abyssal**.

adaptation The process by which an organism changes to fit in with its environment in the course of evolution. An adaptation—a particular characteristic that fits an animal for its way of life.

algae Simple plants and plantlike organisms.

algal Belonging to algae.

ammonite Type of shelled cephalopod mollusk, common as fossils, now extinct.

amphibian Member of group of animals which may live on land as adults, but lay eggs in water that develop through a larval (tadpole) stage.

amphibious Living partly on land, partly in water.

aquatic Living in water.

arthropod Member of group of jointed-legged invertebrate animals, including insects, crustaceans, and trilobites.

asymmetrical Not symmetrical, see **symmetrical**.

baleen Horny plates in a whale's jaw used for filtering food from water.

belemnite Extinct type of cephalopod mollusk.

bivalve Mollusk with a double shell, such as a clam.

blowhole The breathing hole (nostrils) of a whale.

Cambrian A period of the Earth's history from 543 to 490 million years ago.

camouflage Colored, shaped, or with behavior that helps an animal fit in with its surroundings so that it is hard to detect.

carnivore An animal that eats meat.

cartilage Gristle, a material softer than bone, that makes up all or part of the skeleton in some animals.

cephalopod A group of mollusks with well-developed "heads." Cephalopods include squid, octopus, and several extinct groups.

cocoon A protective covering that an animal secretes around itself.

compound eye An eye made up of a large number of sections, or facets, such as that of an insect.

continental shelf A shelf extending from the edge of a continent and covered by a shallow sea.

copepod A type of crustacean.

crustaceans Jointed-legged animals, generally aquatic and breathing with gills. They have a tough external skeleton, and the body is usually divided into a recognizable head, thorax, and abdomen. Crustaceans include crabs, shrimps, copepods, and others.

cyanobacteria Sometimes called blue-greens, these are primitive single-celled organisms. They are among the most ancient known organisms, going back 3,500 million years.

dorsal Of the back. Used to describe the back fins in fish.

echinoderm One of the group of spiny-skinned animals, built to a radially

Amphibian

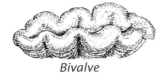

Bivalve

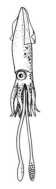

Cephalopod

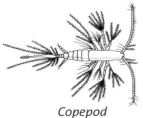

Copepod

symmetrical body plan, that includes starfish and sea urchins.

ecosystem The animals, plants, and other organisms that form an interactive community with their physical surroundings.

enamel The hard substance that coats our teeth. It is also found on some fish scales.

environment The surroundings of an organism.

extinct Describes a type of animal or plant no longer living.

fossil The remains, found in the rocks, of an animal or plant that was once alive.

fossilization The process of becoming a fossil.

gill A thin-skinned organ for breathing in water.

glacial Associated with ice, or glaciers.

hemoglobin The red pigment found in blood that is important for transporting oxygen around the body.

hydrothermal vents Deep volcanic openings on the ocean floor that produce hot water.

immobile Not moving.

impermeable Not allowing water through.

ink sac A bag inside a cephalopod's body full of dark pigment. The pigment may be expelled suddenly to distract an enemy.

insectivore An insect eater.

invertebrate Any animal that does not have a backbone.

keratin The material of which horn, nails, claws, and hair are made.

krill A small crustacean important as food for many sea creatures.

lampshell A brachiopod, one of a group of animals that flourished hundreds of millions of years ago, that now has few survivors.

larva Young stage of some animals, between egg and adult. Plural **larvae**.

lateral line A line along the side of a fish that contains sense organs sensitive to movements in the water.

lobefinned Describes a fish with rather solid fins supported by bones rather like those in our limbs.

mammal Warm-blooded backboned animal that feeds its young on milk. Mammals usually have hair.

marine Relating to the sea.

marsupial Mammals whose young develop in a pouch on the mother's belly, not in a placenta.

migration Regular seasonal movements by animals.

mollusk Invertebrate animal such as a snail or clam, with a soft unsegmented body, usually protected by one or two hard shells.

mosasaur An extinct type of giant aquatic lizard.

myoglobin A dark red pigment found in muscle. Like hemoglobin, it can hold oxygen.

Hydrothermal vents

Invertebrate

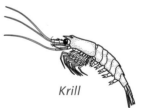
Krill

Mollusk

© DIAGRAM

Plankton

Polyp

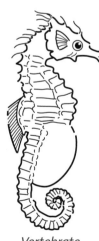

Vertebrate

nasal Of the nose.

parasite An animal that lives on, or inside, another and feeds upon it while the host animal is still alive.

pectoral Of the chest. Used to describe the front pair of fins in fish.

pelvic Of the hip. Used to describe the rear pair of fins in fish.

pigment A chemical that produces a color.

placental Of a mammal in which the young are nourished inside the mother before birth through a blood-filled organ called the placenta.

plankton Organisms, mostly small, that live in the surface layers of the ocean and are carried by the currents.

polyp A single "individual" coral animal within a colony. Also used of solitary sea anemones, etc.

predator An animal that catches and kills other animals for food.

prehensile Grasping. Often used to describe tails that can grasp.

prey An animal that is caught by another for food.

primitive Describes an early member of a group of animals, or one showing characteristics believed to be similar to those of early animals.

radula The tongue of a mollusk, usually covered in tiny horny teeth.

ray-finned Describes a fish like a herring, or other teleost, in which the fins are thin, sometimes transparent, and supported by rays running from the base.

replenish Refill.

reptile A member of the group of animals that are typically land-living, air-breathing, have a scaly skin, and lay shelled eggs.

segmented With a body made up of distinct sections along its length.

sinus A space within the body. It may be filled with air, blood, oil, or other material depending on the animal.

spiracle A hole in front of the gill slits in rays and sharks that can be important in circulating water for breathing.

streamlined Shaped to reduce resistance to movement through water or air.

subarctic Describes regions just outside the Arctic Circle.

swim bladder A balloonlike structure within a fish. In some types it is connected with the gut and may be used to breathe air. In others, this connection is lost, but the swim bladder helps regulate buoyancy.

symmetrical With equal parts. For example, with two sides equal (bilateral symmetry) or similar parts arranged in a ring (radial symmetry).

teleost Member of the modern group of ray-finned bony fishes that makes up the majority of living fish.

venom Poison produced by an animal for killing prey or for defense.

ventral Of the belly or lower underside of an animal.

vertebrate An animal with a backbone.

vibrissae Whiskers that are used to feel the surroundings.

There is a lot of useful information on the internet. There are also many sites that are fun to use. Remember that you may be able to get information on a particular topic by using a search engine such as Google (*http://www.google.com*). Some of the sites that are found in this way may be very useful, others not. Below is a selection of websites related to the material covered by this book. Most are illustrated, and they are mainly of the type that provides useful facts.

Facts On File, Inc. *takes no responsibility for the information contained within these websites. All the sites were accessible as of September 1, 2003.*

AmphibiaWeb
An online database of amphibian biology, and amphibian conservation.
http://elib.cs.berkeley.edu/aw/

The Cephalopod Page
A website on squid, octopuses, and other cephalopods. Includes some advanced material, but also hosts pictures and information on a number of living species. Watch out for the squid-ink cursor.
http://www.dal.ca/~ceph/TCP/

Cetacea
An online resource devoted to whales, dolphins, and porpoises.
http://www.cetacea.org

Crocodilians: Natural History and Conservation
A very detailed resource on crocodiles and their relatives.
http://www.crocodilian.com

Florida Museum of Natural History: Ichthyology
A shark information page with both popular and "serious" material.
http://www.flmnh.ufl.edu/fish/Sharks/sharks.htm

International Marine Mammal Conservation: Pinniped Factsheets
Facts about seals, sea lions, and walruses.
http://www.imma.org/pinnipeds/

Living Lakes
Information on a selection of lakes and wetlands across the world.
http://www.livinglakes.org

Museum of Science, Boston: Oceans Alive!
Facts on the oceans, and links to various (and variable) other sites.
http://www.mos.org/oceans/planet/

Museum Victoria: Prehistoric Life
A good summary of the anatomy and fossil history of many groups of invertebrates.
http://www.museum.vic.gov.au/prehistoric/time/

Oceans of Kansas: Plesiosaurs
An informative page on plesiosaurs, with many illustrations, photographs, and links.
http://www.oceansofkansas.com/plesio2.html

Oxford University, Museum of Natural History: Fossils
An introduction to fossils, including some sea invertebrates not covered in this book.
http://www.oum.ox.ac.uk/children/fossils/kidsgeol.htm

Sea and Sky: The Sea
A colorful website on sea exploration, animals, and more.
http://www.seasky.org/sea.html

Sea Turtle Survival League/Caribbean Conservation Corporation
A factual site on sea turtles and their protection.
http://www.cccturtle.org

Turtle Trax
A website devoted to marine turtles.
http://www.turtles.org

UCB, Museum of Paleontology: Amphibians
An introduction to amphibians, both living and extinct.
http://www.ucmp.berkeley.edu/vertebrates/tetrapods/amphibintro.html

UCB, Museum of Paleontology: Coelacanths
The latest news on coelacanths, including a living species discovered near Indonesia.
http://www.ucmp.berkeley.edu/vertebrates/coelacanth/coelacanths.html

UCB, Museum of Paleontology: Ichthyosaurs
The world of the ichthyosaurs.
http://www.ucmp.berkeley.edu/people/motani/ichthyo/

UCB, Museum of Paleontology: Vendian Animals
Photographs of and information about some of the earliest animal fossils. The site includes links to other groups and other periods of the Earth's history.
http://www.ucmp.berkeley.edu/vendian/critters.html

University of Kentucky, Geological Survey: The Devonian Period
A list of links to material on lungfishes, other early fishes, and the first tetrapods.
http://www.uky.edu/KGS/education/Devonian.html